Lifechanges

Also by Judith Hatch Shapiro

Son of the Revolution (with Liang Heng)
After the Nightmare (with Liang Heng)
Cold Winds, Warm Winds (with Liang Heng)

Also by Joan Hatch Lennox (Joan Shapiro)

Communities of the Alone

Lifechanges

HOW WOMEN CAN MAKE
COURAGEOUS CHOICES

Joan Hatch Lennox
Judith Hatch Shapiro

Crown Publishers, Inc., New York

Published by Crown Publishers, Inc., 201 East 50th Street,
New York, New York 10022

CROWN is a trademark of Crown Publishers, Inc.

Manufactured in the United States of America

Library of Congress Cataloging-in-Publication Data
Lennox, Joan Hatch.
    Lifechanges : how women can make courageous choices/Joan
    Hatch Lennox and Judith Hatch Shapiro.—1st ed.
        p.   cm.
    Includes bibliographical references (p.   ).
    1. Women—Psychology. 2. Self-actualization (Psychology)
I. Shapiro, Judith, 1953–   . II. Title
HQ1206.L429   1990
155.6'33—dc20   90-1712
                                                              CIP

ISBN 0-517-57686-4

Book Design by Shari deMiskey

10   9   8   7   6   5   4   3   2   1

First Edition

We dedicate this book to each other

One is not born, but rather becomes a woman.

SIMONE DE BEAUVOIR

Contents

Preface

LIKE MOST BOOKS, THIS ONE WAS WRITTEN FOR PERSONAL REA-
sons. We both recently divorced, changed communities, developed new intimate relationships and circles of friends, and
refocused our work. Joan quietly ended a thirty-year marriage,
moved to Massachusetts, helped build herself a house in the
woods, began to explore Latin America, and prepared for her
retirement from Smith College. Judith and her Chinese husband and coauthor divorced amicably; she moved from New
York to Philadelphia, bought an old stone house, and made
the transition from a joint career into her own. This book
reflects these thresholds and paths of change and our sharing
with each other of how we traversed them; the greatest gift of
our work together has been our partnership as mother and
daughter.

We recognize that inner growth changes behavior. But in

recent years we have both learned new respect for the power of change in the externals of our lives, as accidents of opportunity and people became forces that shaped our internal transformations. We discovered that small, unthreatening, even arbitrary external shifts were steps toward the more difficult process of inner change. Making minor changes in noncrucial areas helped us get in touch with our power to act and led us to be bolder in tackling difficult issues. We attempt here to share this simple but very important insight and to help you explore how you might use it in your lives.

Writing about and for women has been a special privilege. We have at times felt in conversation with you. The choice to make this a book for women only was not a simple one, however, for men and women share the same issues, if not always the same language, way of thinking, or approach to change.

Many women shared their stories with us and, through us, with you. They told us of fears and hesitations, of seeking the subtle balance point for changes that were not so ambitious that anxiety overwhelmed excitement and pleasure, not so small that they were merely trivial. These women risked change through soul-searching redefinitions of themselves, through job, education, and community changes, through hard work on deepening their relationships, and through the literal expansion of their horizons by traveling the world. Some remained frozen in obsolete patterns or in inflexible life situations because they had not found the right starting places for change. We have ensured their privacy by altering our accounts of them in minor ways.

Sometimes people told us stories of transformation impelled by trauma—Frances, who lost her only daughter and son-in-law in a car accident yet after a time filled the void with deeply satisfying volunteer work; seventy-eight-year-old Eileen, who became a well-known quilt maker after she was confined to a wheelchair. Others told of success born of the will to change and grow—Jenny, who learned to drive late, at thirty-two, and took a job as a bus driver; Lisa, who finished college in her forties and became a professor. These stories inspire us and help us discard the notion that we are already fully formed adults who might just as well not try to make changes.

More deeply interesting than these outcomes, however, is the process by which the women arrived at their transformations. Behind every such tale lies a difficult struggle with inertia and uncertainty. There were tentative moves, mistakes, and setbacks. Often, self-doubt was overcome with the support of others who offered comfort and encouragement when the going was especially difficult. Then came the slow metamorphosis: I am becoming able to be contentedly alone, to say no, to enjoy exercising, to spend happier time with my parents—in short, I am different.

We wish you, too, broad and inviting thresholds, and a challenging and joyful exploration of the paths of your choosing.

Lifechanges

I · Getting Started

All changes, even the most longed for, have their melancholy; for what we leave behind us is a part of ourselves; we must die to one life before we can enter another.

ANATOLE FRANCE

IMAGINE YOURSELF IN A DOORWAY, STANDING ON THE THRESHOLD and looking out. Paths fan outward before you like the spokes of a wheel. These are the paths of change. You will soon decide which of them to choose at this moment of your life and how far you will venture down it. The only thing that is certain is that you will step off the threshold, from stillness to action, from hesitation to decision. Whether you take a small footstep or a great stride, your choice will create energy for the next. Then many footsteps follow, one to the next, until once again you stand poised on a threshold of change.

Some women are lucky enough to be relatively content, their ideals closely matching their lives. But most of us are at a threshold in at least one area. We stand poised, trying to muster the courage and sense the right timing for the passage through to some place that we cannot see clearly and do not fully understand.

Welcome or not, change is often the one constant in our

lives. We are ceaselessly developing and adjusting, as shifting external circumstances and the natural momentum of growth propel us toward the next synthesis. We are constantly looking for the fragile balance between our need for stability and continuity and our thirst for stimulation and challenge.

Sometimes we get stuck. Indecisiveness becomes a habit; an unsatisfying situation seems immutable; the wrong partner, job, or home freezes in on us. Past selves haunt us like ghosts, obsolete forms with no purpose. An insistent tic of discontent is a reminder of some underdeveloped part of the self, some unexplored talent or experience, some unrealized wish. Years ago, when women had fewer choices, we might quietly have accepted our lot. But now change of our own choice and making is possible and desirable, as more and more of us are in a position to take charge of our lives.

A conscious decision to change does not necessarily imply that we must tear up a comfortable life or a satisfactory partnership; the changes we seek may mean differences in the quality of what we do rather than in external structures. Change does, however, require looking more closely at those areas in which we are ambivalent or unsatisfied.

In any area, from the tiny to the enormous, from getting a haircut to getting a divorce, change implies a push away from the familiar rut and a pull toward a new pattern. Motion must overcome inertia: this truism we enact in dozens of ways every day. There is a tension between staying in bed and getting up, between washing the dishes right away or delaying. So, too, the decision to change some area of our lives needs both the push of dissatisfaction and the pull of possible pleasure and accomplishment. The change points, so deeply personal, must have resonance for us, and they must be possible within the framework of our own life circumstances. The means and the energy must be there, and the moment must be ripe.

If change is forced upon us from the outside, we can work toward making even the most unwelcome turns of events into opportunities for new experience and growth. Sometimes such changes descend through catastrophe, as we are suddenly widowed, lose jobs, a child or grandchild falls seriously ill, an investment disappears, or a house burns. Or they come more gradually, through the slow aging and increased dependency of parents, the indecisive dissolution of a marriage, the inexorable approach of retirement, the creeping loss of physical stamina and memory. Of course, the external changes may also be welcome ones: a graduation, the birth of a child, a marriage. These changes, too, may present unexpected challenges, raising the need now for our involvement in creating other changes we did not anticipate.

For some of us, the challenge may lie in psychological jungles. Hidden fears and motivations may be shaping our lives and determining our choices. If we work now on naming and describing them, we will vastly increase our options and control of the future. We may wish to explore other inner arenas: build a new type of relationship, learn to stand our ground, forgive a long hostility, or relinquish a hunger for accumulation. One could argue that a change in basic character is not realistic for adults. And for some, this may be true. But with clear insight into a trait or pattern we deeply want to change—jealousy, passivity, fussiness, stinginess, reclusiveness, impatience—we can alter some of our superficial behavior. Gradually that behavior can inform the deeper structures of our personalities. If a change we deeply seek proves out of reach, or a difficult trait is stubbornly resistant, we can always turn to a counselor.

We invite you here, then, with full respect for your flexibility, power, and will to survive, to identify aspects of your life in which change may be desirable and possible.

Together, we begin by examining such immediately accessible areas as our physical selves and our arrangement of personal space. We continue with an examination of attitudes toward money, new intellectual and manual challenges, travel, and solitude. We conclude with the more difficult tasks of changing our relationships with friends and lovers and with our parents. At the end of each chapter we suggest a series of "minitasks," some small, some fun, some difficult, among which to choose as an aid to defining and exploring areas for possible change. We also offer a short list of suggested readings to take you further into those subjects that attract you most.

If you are to gain the most from this book, you should consider keeping a journal to keep track of your new beginnings, the obstacles you encounter, and the ways in which you are overcoming them. Or write down your thoughts and reactions here in the margins. Your comments can be quick notes or long letters to yourself. Writing down thoughts, however briefly, has a magical quality of clarifying inner confusion. The writing will be a signal to yourself of your seriousness and, with time, a reminder of the progress you have made. Years from now you will have a record of your journey that can be a source of remembrance and pleasure.

If you are to change, then all the strength, wisdom, and know-how of your past must be gathered in and concentrated on yourself. Think now for a few minutes of what you are about to do in this next, exciting and unknown period of your life. What do you really want to explore, or learn, or be now, at this fresh moment? Where do your instincts tell you that dissatisfactions lie and potential rewards await? Begin, if you can, with the following resolutions:

1. *I will acknowledge, in writing, the important areas of myself that have no voice in my current life.* This is the first step: to see what in yourself is now impoverished.

2. *I will become aware, impartially and lovingly, of what those closest to me can and cannot give me.* The second step: to look again at the others in your life. You may wish to deepen your relationships, to make new ones, to adjust the amount of time you spend with others and how you apportion it, or to leave some unsatisfying relationships behind altogether.

4

3. *I will try to recognize in myself those patterned responses that no longer satisfy me.* The third step: to examine your habits and rituals. You may, for example, have an ancient impulse to start cooking as soon as grown children show up; a tendency to set huge tasks and then berate yourself for the failure to complete them; a frustrating pattern of trying to harvest love by centering energy on another person.

4. *I will commit myself to a path of deepening inner honesty about my feelings. I will become more aware of unwelcome or unmanageable responses, such as anger, loneliness, fear, envy, or whatever I tend most to push away from myself.* The fourth step: to admit what you really feel. Acknowledging these feelings in your journal does not mean that you must act on them or express them in public, but rather that it will be a relief if you let yourself stop pretending.

5. *I will find small steps to approach big problems and new challenges. I will explore my newborn impulses gently and avoid confronting difficult issues head-on.* The fifth step: to find a way to begin that is truly possible and not frightening. If you try to think all at once about everything that needs to be changed, you will probably feel overwhelmed and incapacitated. For most people, taking a short course for no credit, rather than a full semester with four courses, is the best way to explore going back to school; one visit to a health or exercise club for a look can be less overwhelming than purchasing a full year's membership with its prospect of a daily workout.

6. *I will try not to load "should"s and "ought"s into my contemplation of change. Instead, I will replace them with "want to"s.* The sixth step: to emphasize the positive aspects of change. Think about how you want to try new things because you are curious, interested, and stimulated. Change, for example, the self-critical "I should drink less coffee" to "I want to be calmer as I go through my day" or "I have to get rid of this ugly fat" to "I'm looking forward to feeling strong as I bicycle to work."

7. *I will accept and forgive my false steps, errors in judgment, or attempts that prove too ambitious for a beginner on a new path.* The seventh step: to recognize that change does not come as a steady progression; the pattern is usually in uneven steps. Dissonance, chaos, and reorganization are necessary stages toward transformation to a new stability. If you need to, you can retreat and prepare to try again.

8. *I will trust that my active struggle for different life solutions, roles, and self-concepts will lead eventually to new integrations, relationships, and freedoms.* The eighth step: to acknowledge that these new roles will not necessarily be happier or more peaceful than those of the past, but they will certainly be stimulating and fresh.

We all know women like Karen, who is deeply dissatisfied with her present life but, because she cannot conceive of alternatives, dares not acknowledge her unhappiness even to herself. She is a physically active, attractive woman, an army wife who once seriously considered a career as a clarinetist. Her husband retired several years ago and has become quite demanding and reclusive. Her four children have large families who visit regularly, and the house is often full of boisterous activity. Karen is always available, nurturing, and seemingly serene.

The truth of this rosy picture is that much of the time Karen feels she is little better than a maid, left at home to clean up while everyone else goes off on adventures in the outside world. She rarely makes it to rehearsal with her beloved church wind instrument ensemble because she believes she must be available to baby-sit, cook, and clean at a moment's notice. Although she would never admit that she is resentful, she sometimes finds herself unaccountably depressed, wishing that everybody would go home and leave her in peace.

Getting Started

Karen cannot imagine what her life would be like if she changed her lifelong pattern of putting the needs of others ahead of her own. She fears, undoubtedly irrationally, that if she said no or set limits, she would drive her family away and lose their love and affection. The thought of an empty house seems far more unattractive than whatever "small" sacrifices she must make to keep everyone happy.

Like Karen, most of us tend to remain stuck because of the dread and uncertainty of unknown places, people, and outcomes. It is difficult to trade a familiar, if flawed, pattern for a hypothetical future for which there are no guarantees. One of our most important tasks together, then, is to find ways of getting in touch with the energy and courage for that leap into the unknown.

Another task is to review our self-knowledge. Many of us have needlessly limiting images of our personalities, for example, and these hold us back from making changes that we may deeply want. "I can't keep a secret," we say. "I have no sense of humor," "I'm a fraud; I'm not what people think I am." Often these are self-fulfilling notions that germinated early in life, perhaps because a single experience was allowed to grow into psychological reality. Some of these self-portraits have a partial truth, some do not. They can be powerfully destructive, especially during major life changes like illness, breakups, widowhood, or job loss, when we need to draw upon all of our best and most flexible resources.

Our dreams of change are also often blocked by internal myths about our abilities. Many of us believe, for example, that we are no good at learning languages, that we have a bad sense of direction, that we have little sense of style, or that we are not athletic. Almost all of us do a dance of denial and adjustment around such areas of anxiety. These firmly entrenched and often ill-founded notions stand in the way of fuller lives for ourselves.

Kim, for example, is a successful writer, divorced and now living alone. She is continually productive, well known as an essayist, book reviewer, and political commentator. Yet she carries the weight of a self-perception that it is her brother and not she who is the creative member of the family. She sees herself as unimaginative, a view that has impeded her whenever the opportunity for "creative" writing has arisen, even if it is merely a description of a person or locale. She knows that her analytical abilities are only part of her talent and fantasizes about signing up for a course in creative writing as a way of circumventing childhood roles. The idea of actually doing so is terribly frightening, however, and she is nowhere close to taking action. She must find a less threatening way to begin.

If we want to change, we will want to become more familiar with our favorite tactics of avoidance and delay. It may be helpful to think about procrastination as being of three types:

1. The avoidance of unpleasant, tedious, but not threatening tasks.

2. The avoidance of tasks or actions that make us anxious because they remind us of our less-than-competent or confident selves.

3. The avoidance of solving creative problems because the solutions are gestating within us and are not yet ripe for translation into action.

In the first kind of procrastination, simple avoidance of unpleasant chores such as washing the kitchen floor, ironing shirts, or changing the kitty litter, we usually substitute more pleasant activities such as going out or watching TV.

In the second kind of procrastination, the avoidance of anxiety, we often substitute tasks that are tedious and get a lot done: suddenly the idea of washing the kitchen floor seems far more attractive than finishing a term paper. Often we are not aware that we are putting something off, or why. Then it is the last minute, and we can find no other excuse. Suffering, we complete the dreaded task—with its reward of relief, pride, and, perhaps, ruefulness at all the aggravation we put ourselves through.

In the third type of procrastination, we are searching for a form and a solution. We feel remote from the task, while knowing that it will at some time become intimate and clear. Such creative procrastination, so familiar to artists, seems less acceptable when it involves an agonizingly complicated letter, a financial decision, or a trip that requires risk and courage. Yet the answer to a staffing problem at work or the composition of an important letter of reference, not to speak of the creative process in art, may require time for sorting out and cannot be forced. Although we may feel we are procrastinating, and even torment ourselves for the delay, we are in fact mulling our way toward resolution of the preoccupying problem.

Interestingly, the most skilled procrastinators among us are often also the most dedicated perfectionists. The risk of failure is greater because the standards that must be met are so exacting. Perhaps we fear that we may be unable to live up to our own high expectations or even that the idea or resolution will never come. Our delay is a complex form of fear of failure.

Like most of us, Suzanna is quite familiar with all three types of procrastination. A weaver of large rugs that she sells at country fairs, she upholsters furniture for her everyday living. One of her procrastinations belongs to the "unpleasant task" variety. Sewing buttons back on after finishing a chair or sofa is a detailed job she dislikes because the placement of the button has to be exact and the long needle is clumsy to handle. Furniture that is completed except for the buttons remains in her storeroom for weeks, often until customers inquire about the source of the delay. At the avoidance-of-anxiety level, she postpones composing her monthly ads for the regional trade journal because she is always afraid of having either too much or too little business, and she has trouble sounding the right note of authority without feeling she is making hollow boasts in the eyes of her peers. Suzanna procrastinates artistically whenever she is planning a new rug. She takes weeks to turn over patterns and textures in her mind. This is when she is most productive in the house: she redecorates and rearranges, playing with color and light as an indirect way of approaching her deeper aesthetic decision.

Take a few minutes now, if you wish, to write down your own patterns with the three levels of procrastination.

- What are the tasks that you avoid at each level?

- What are the most common things you do while you are putting them off?

- Are your favorite substitutes generally productive or self-destructive?

- Have you ever procrastinated to a really destructive point, so that you undercut yourself in an important way (at work, for example, or on a deadline)?

- Are there more positive ways to procrastinate than those you typically use now?

If you are an inveterate procrastinator, here is a common but very effective technique for overcoming inertia: Make a list of things to do, in any order, including both very important and extremely trivial things. Write down even those chores that are utterly routine, like depositing a check or buying new light bulbs. Make it a habit to cross off one or more items every day, without being self-critical if only the easiest tasks are accomplished. Mood, inner strength, energy, and momentum have much to do with what you will be able to accomplish. Make a new list every time the old one gets messy or you feel a need to get a handle on your life; the simple act of rewriting the list can give you a sense of gaining control.

As Jeannine discovered, the day will come when that terrible item you have been transferring from list to list suddenly seems like just one more thing to take care of. Jeannine's husband left her and two small children for an affair with one of his students. For months Jeannine felt that there was little reason to live. She spent days in bed, barely taking care of the children and putting on thirty pounds. Then time passed, and she began to pull out of her depression. She found a lawyer who helped her attend to the legal and practical aspects of the separation.

Even after the divorce, however, there was one thing she could not bring herself to do: change the mailbox reading "The Williamses." "New sign" had its place on every list of things to do. Then, about six months after the divorce, when she was returning home after her new aerobics class, she impulsively stopped in at a hardware store for a new mailbox and painted on her maiden name with nail polish. Writing down that entry on each of her lists had been an important way of slowly assimilating the idea of her new identity.

Another tactic for dealing with procrastination over tough goals is to make plans that force you to keep them. Eileen, for example, had a difficult time letting go of a mahogany table she had agreed to give to her husband during their divorce discussions. Although she had always disliked the table, she found herself making excuses to avoid scheduling its removal. She understood that it symbolized the family life they had shared, and that her resistance was to the idea that her married life was really over. Finally she found a way to outsmart herself: she volunteered her home for a local charity's annual cocktail party, knowing that the living room could not possibly hold everyone with the huge table there. In the excitement of preparing for the party with her friends, she found herself eager for the movers' arrival, and their departure with the table was even a relief.

So far we have emphasized the positive aspects of change. Sometimes, however, we need to display caution rather than action. We impetuously push our way through major decisions, as though we might be scared to do whatever it is if we didn't ride on our reckless impulse. The results are not always what we really wanted.

Anita had wanted for a long time to build a nest and raise a family. She fell in love and very soon moved to the other side of the country, where she bought a house in equal shares with her boyfriend Tim. Overwhelmed by the new financial responsibilities and the terrifying fact of commitment, Tim opted out of the relationship less than six months after they moved into the house. Although Anita had few friends in the new city and only the promise of a full-time job, she felt unwilling to be uprooted again so quickly and decided to spend her small inheritance on buying him out. With a sense of desperation and urgency fueled by her grief at the end of the relationship, her belief that somehow the new challenge would be interesting, and perhaps a vengeful desire to possess the house he so loved but could not afford, she persuaded him to accept her offer rather than fix the place up and put it on the market.

Soon after the transfer, however, real estate took a nosedive and the house proved to have a major radon problem. Far away from close friends and relatives, saddled with a major responsibility that she had few skills to handle, and uncertain that she would be able to meet her financial commitments, Anita is slowly finding a way out of her ill-considered venture and regretting her eagerness for change at any price.

The simplest approach to change is to begin in an area of your immediate daily life in which you know you can do better. Let's suppose your early-morning routine has too little time in it for personal grooming: skin, hair, and teeth routines are performed in a pleasureless rush. You always seem to leave the house breathless and unsettled. Or perhaps you stay in bed much longer than you feel good about, and each day begins with a languid, diffuse passivity that somehow sets the tone for the whole day.

Identify your wish to change: "I would like my day to begin

with an active serenity." Then create a manageable new time discipline, a pact to wake up and get out of bed at a specific time. The payoff will be immediate, because you will feel you are taking steps to control this small problem, and a new habit may take root. Of course, you may discover that tried-and-true ways work best for you, but only by forcing yourself to experiment will you know for sure.

In the beginnings just suggested, the search for discipline and routine is a theme. But if this is difficult and fraught with resistance for one person, it may be a breeze for someone else. Perhaps you want to become more flexible, less clock- and schedule-bound. Then the task becomes to allow yourself to deviate, to mix things up, not to do the proverbial laundry on Monday. Whatever your most tenacious patterns are, if they have stopped functioning well for you, they are candidates for scrutiny.

As we prepare to look more closely at the areas of our lives that may be ripe for change, we must remember that we do not change in a social vacuum. There are husbands, parents, lovers, friends, or children who may resist our evolution. They, too, are enamored of the familiar and will be upset by new attitudes and activities, especially when these mean departures from such common female patterns as preparing meals, being home to serve and clean, and being available for evening, weekend, and vacation activities. Husbands and lovers, in particular, can interpret our taking more time or space for ourselves as hostility. A woman in the process of making changes is very often seen as a puzzling and unsettling person or as aggressive and man-hating. Even an adult child no longer living at home can feel angry and unloved by this newly self-absorbed mother who is going off to Mexico. For many women, other people's disapproval is frightening and confrontations are difficult; we often find it easier to back down than to continue in a course we see as inducing anger or unhappiness.

We will therefore want to include the people in our households and, if possible, make them allies. We will want to help them by alerting them in advance to the changes that may affect their lives. "For the next few months I won't be able to baby-sit for you on Monday or Wednesday nights, because I've decided to take that French course I told you about." "Since I have so much less time this year, let's ask one of the children if we can have Thanksgiving at his house. It would be a pleasant change, and I could bring the turkey." "I'm thinking about taking a small amount of money and investing it for myself, to learn about financial management." We must talk about what we are trying to do, and talk about it early and often. We may find ourselves changing in more and more profound ways; if we want our living arrangement to continue peacefully, we must begin early to share as much of our inner lives and dreams as possible.

Finally, we will want to resist the temptation to rip too deeply into our habitual fabric, to change too many things at once. We may need much time and patience to incorporate the changes and make them truly a part of our lives. Every change involves its good-byes, and we need to give ourselves time not only to bring in the new, but also to say farewell to what we are leaving behind.

□

MINITASKS

These minitasks are an opportunity for you to begin putting into practice some of the ideas and suggestions from the preceding chapter. They are meant to be used as you wish: Try one or two; do them all or none at all.

1 ▪ Buy a journal or blank book that pleases you aesthetically and practically and is small enough to carry around in your purse. On page one, isolate and name one issue or change point in your current life that has brought you to reading this book. As you gently work into the tasks of the book, commit

yourself to looking at this area deeply, including both the anxieties and potential for growth. Make a conscious resolution to be open to change.

2 ▪ On another page, write down five minor but unproductive habits. Choose just one, and make a compact with yourself to change it gently, for just one week. Examples:

If you go to the store without a list, only to find when you return home that you have forgotten the cat food, paper towels, and olive oil and, because of the cat, have to go back again, put a pad with an attached pen on the refrigerator door and use it faithfully until your next shopping trip.

If you tend toward overscrupulousness and wash dishes every time the sink has one or two items in it, try waiting until after mealtimes and see how that feels.

If your bookkeeping is haphazard and chronically late, try paying each bill on the day it arrives.

Tell the others in your household about your plan ahead of time, ask for encouragement and support, and show appreciation for their help in getting you to stick to it. At the end of the first week, write down what it was like and choose one more small area you would like to change.

3 ▪ In your journal, divide into columns the things you can't change (for example, where you live, your current job, the timing of your retirement, or your husband's Parkinson's disease) and the things you can change (such as the way the furniture is arranged, your poor attendance at an exercise class, the garage that services your car so poorly, the no-longer-enjoyable volunteer work with the Girl Scouts). As you write things down in list form, you will begin to see one or more starting places, however small. Choose just one, no matter how trivial. Act on it, talking about it first with those it will affect.

4 ▪ Write down, with a short phrase, three concrete tasks that you are procrastinating doing (calling your mother, preparing your income tax, asking your neighbor to dinner, hemming the new skirt, scrubbing the shower). Under each item, find words for why you *want to*, not *should*, do this. In parallel, find words for why you might be resisting doing it. For example:

Task: Neighbors to Dinner

Why I want to: Good relationships give me a sense of community. The Smiths have been kind to me, especially in emergencies, and I went to their house for a party last month.

Why I don't want to: They are a bit "heavy" socially, and I can't stand their political views. We are better at doing things together than sitting talking. I am only a medium-confident cook, and I am nervous about how the meal would turn out. I would really need to clean house beforehand.

Write down tactics for solving this problem. For example, for dinner with the Smiths it might be "Plan an active meal: fondue, barbecue, smorgasbord. It should be something for which I can make almost all of the preparations in advance. Or make it pot luck. Invite another guest or two."

Out of the three tasks, pick the one for which the "tactic" seems most inviting, and do it.

5 ▪ Invent your own minitask, with a creative, unthreatening solution that can be approached in small steps. For example:

Perhaps you are critical of your tendency to neglect friends or relatives who are far away. Your active network of people is in the neighborhood, even though others have a far deeper and longer claim to your loyalty and affection. You are embarrassed when you get cards or phone calls with a faintly curt tone, but you feel you probably deserve it. The task you set for yourself might look like this: Look through your address book and draw up a list of three people whom you care about and want news of. Think about your relationship with each one as you are making the list: the best parts of your history together, the uncomfortable aspects, the things in your life that you do and don't want to share with them, the things about them that you do and don't like. Ask yourself why you have not made contact. Is there any awkwardness or embarrassment? If so, why? Does it explain your inertia? Feel free to cross some people off: you have no respect or affection for Uncle Hal, so off he goes. Then put the list up in plain view, with addresses, near your desk. Buy a packet of small, attractive note cards and every few days write just *one* person a brief, newsy, warm note. Your sense of satisfaction may surprise you; any responses will be a secondary reward.

6 ▪ Identify one "big" issue in your life and see if you can find an oblique way of approaching it. If you are deeply intimidated by your boss, for example, and are tired of the many unre-solved issues between you (non-work-related demands, unpre-dictable workloads, inadequate work space), instead of gearing up for a major complaint session, try writing her/him a short, informal note suggesting an alternative approach to one rela-tively simple issue.

7 ▪ Try to identify and write down two occasions in the last week in which you were less than honest with yourself. Try to recognize if you have lied to yourself about your anger (toward the child who forgot to call you on your birthday), guilt (to-ward your mother, who has to live in a nursing home but says she would rather move in with you), ambivalence (toward a co-worker whose pet dog you refused to look after during her vacation), sexual attraction (toward someone off limits, unat-tainable, or socially inappropriate), or something else, big or small. Then write down how these feelings emerged. Why would you rather not recognize them?

8 ▪ Write down one trait or family myth about yourself that you doubt is really true and that you want to change, such as finicky eating, clumsiness, bad driving, or tactlessness. Try to identify where it came from, what pieces of family history made it stick. Put up a small sign to the contrary, saying, for example, "I'll eat anything" or "I'm a good driver."

9 ▪ Write down three tasks now hanging over your head that belong to the "avoidance of unpleasant or tedious tasks" type of procrastination: scrubbing the refrigerator or garbage can; cleaning out your desk; canceling a magazine subscription. When do you become aware that they must be attended to? What do you usually do instead? Now write down what circumstances finally lead you to stop putting them off.

10 ▪ Write down three tasks of the "avoidance of tasks or actions that make you anxious" variety: writing a term paper; paying the bills; preparing to give a talk in front of other people. How do you spend your time avoiding these things? When do you finally stop putting them off, and why? How close to the final deadline do you let yourself come?

11 ▪ Write down three tasks that are of the "artistic procrastination" type: writing a long, thoughtful letter to a friend; redoing the bathroom in new colors; beginning to knit a sweater with a design you haven't yet determined. Don't crucify yourself for the delay; uncritically allow yourself to appreciate and become more aware of your process of intuitive preparation.

2 · Nests and Boundaries

I dwell in Possibility—
A fairer House than Prose—
More numerous of Windows—
Superior—for Doors.

EMILY DICKINSON

JOY GREW UP IN A TRADITIONAL SMALL TOWN IN THE MIDWEST. Her father managed the local bank; her mother kept an orderly home. When Joy married the accountant of a local factory, she and her new husband were eager to please their parents and show off to their friends. They dressed conservatively, bought a small house and decorated it, invited other young couples over for barbecues, mowed the lawn and planted roses.

When Joy's husband died in an industrial accident when she was twenty-six, there was no more point to the *Better Homes & Gardens* life they had led. Joy sold the house, divested herself of cherished possessions, and drove to Colorado, where her best girlfriend from college had settled.

As a child Joy had been fascinated with animals but was never allowed to have pets because they were "dirty." In her marriage, she had been afraid of the damage they might do to her upholstery. Released from these constraints, Joy now found a job at an animal petting farm for children.

Living in a new circle of far more casual, outdoorsy friends, Joy gradually let go of her extreme tidiness. At work the animals climbed all over her and she had to give up her fussiness about clothes. She found herself acquiring things secondhand and giving them away to friends who liked them. She had casual, paper-plate pickup meals in her second-floor duplex apartment that once would have astonished her: guests sitting on the floor, helping themselves to whatever they needed from the refrigerator, running out for more beer if there wasn't enough. Her formerly strict sense of boundaries and possessiveness, so appropriate to the life-style she and her husband had shared, now seemed meaningless.

We all construct zones of protection around ourselves, familiar areas stamped with our personal histories, preferences, and habits. How we express and even defend the limits of our symbolic spaces varies immensely from person to person. Some build thick walls of security and invest them with great energy and feeling. They protect their privacy fiercely, jealously guard their possessions, or defend their time as inviolate. Others are far more casual. They may not value private space or have difficulty recognizing intrusion until it is too late; the edges of their sense of possession may be blurred by generosity.

Our clothing, purses, living spaces, luggage, and cars are extensions of ourselves; their boundaries define what is ours and what lies beyond. Joy discovered that in a different stage and situation in her life, her sense of these boundaries shifted. For you, too, there may be a time when you care a great deal about your clothing and objects and put much energy into acquiring and protecting them; at some other point you may be simplifying and divesting or acquiring only things that can be given away, loaned, broken, or lost without regret. You may wish now, as you contemplate the possibilities of change in your life, to experiment with shifting your boundaries, increasing or decreasing your sense of mine and thine, self and other.

CLOTHING

Clothes are the first, most intimate boundary between ourselves and the outside world. They may be primarily simple extensions of the skin; they may be most important as ways of keeping a formal distance between the self and others; or they may be mainly costumes, ways of actively playing with perceptions.

Fran, an office manager for a small investment firm, favors tweed skirts and matching sweaters; a subtle and tastefully tied scarf and well-made leather purse completes the sensible, pleasant, and comfortable image she wishes to convey. Even at home, when alone, she tends to dress in matching tops and slacks, as if always prepared to meet the public. For her, dressing is a responsibility, part of her professional identity: her primary consideration is making her persona express her competence as a member of a team.

Hannah is single and lives on a farm. She has lived a rural life always and has a tough, do-it-yourself independence combined with an ability to extend warm hospitality to neighbors in the form of great, spreading picnics and celebrations. She raises goats and manufactures small but choice wheels of goat cheese. Her daily outfit is jeans, workshirt, and a lumber jacket with deep pockets. Although she remembers to wear red during hunting season, colors are usually matters of complete indifference; her main consideration is that the fabrics of her clothes be tough enough to withstand the assault of nuzzling, sharp-hoofed goats.

Lilly puts a great deal of time into her appearance. A tall, willowy college teacher in a theater department, she expresses her wit and sense of costume through ensembles that emphasize the drape and texture of interesting fabrics. She has hundreds of quirky earrings that set off her very black, straight hair and smooth, translucent skin. For Lilly, dressing is an important area of self-expression, even an art: selecting from a range of different images each day means playing different characters in the world that is her stage.

Most of us swing among these three attitudes toward clothes, emphasizing utility, professional image, and costume to different degrees. We are more or less conscious of the impression we make on others, and we vary as to the amount of pleasure we take in clothes, the amount of money we spend, and the degree to which we change our wardrobes according to current fashion.

Which of these attitudes is most like your own?

- Is choosing what to wear a practical duty for you, the adoption of an appropriate uniform?

- Do you see clothes as utilitarian, keeping you warm or keeping you decent in public?

- Are clothes a pleasurable dress-up game, a form of self-expression?

The purse, too, is a powerful extension of ourselves. Its size, shape, appearance, and, above all, contents reveal much about who we are. For most of us, the purse may be, among other things, a desk (address book, pen, note pad), drugstore (aspirin, tissues, throat lozenges, estrogen pills), beauty parlor (nail file, comb, makeup, mirror, perfume), bank (money, credit cards, checks, deposit slips), and closet (panty hose, exercise clothes, towel). For some, purses hold vices: chocolate bars, cigarettes, or tranquilizers. They are among the vehicles by which we negotiate our relationship to our community. Crucially, too, they function as legal representations of our selves, formalized, notarized, and permitted: they hold driver's licenses, senior citizens' cards, health insurance IDs, and membership cards.

Consider now your own purse:

- Is it primarily a statement of your professional role?

- Do you care most about its uses as a bank, pharmacy, and beauty parlor?

- Is it a decorative accessory, a completion of your outfit?

- Is it all of these at once? Or does its role change at different times?

Attitudes about lending and borrowing clothing, shoes, and purses differ, too. These feelings can tell us much about how strict our sense of personal boundaries is.

For Mary, borrowing and lending is an unpleasant idea. All her life her attractiveness has been an important part of her self-awareness, first emphasized by her mother, who dressed her carefully in frilly dresses with socks and ribbons to match. All of teenage Mary's baby-sitting money went for clothes; it was important to her to be first to own the latest fashions, and she loved to show off things that nobody else had. Married and a mother, she continued to dress meticulously, feeling that her sense of style set her apart from the rest of the world, and she was acutely aware of how proud her husband was of her appearance. Now that she's older and living on a careful budget, her beautiful clothes act as a shield against the oncoming of age. She works hard to keep her weight down so that she can continue to wear her fine wardrobe, taking aerobics classes and paying strict attention to her diet. For Mary, lending clothes would be a dilution of her person; it would never occur to her to offer.

At the other end of the continuum there is Agatha, a sophisticated, lifelong city dweller. As a child she fought against pretty clothes, tearing and dirtying them. She now chooses clothes for comfort and washability, remaining as an adult very active and a bit untidy. She gets real pleasure from lending and borrowing, feeling it brings her closer to others. She encourages her same-size daughter to wear her clothes, seeing this as a symbol of the intimacy between them. She is sometimes taken aback when she asks to borrow something and finds that others are not nearly as enthusiastic about such transactions as she.

Most of us will or won't borrow and lend clothes, depending

on the situation, person, and emotional investment in the garment. We are either glad to see someone wearing something of ours or worry about getting it back; we enjoy wearing a borrowed item as a reminder of someone else, or we reject the idea of wearing something that is not ours alone.

Some have strong feelings, either positive or negative, about wearing the clothes of a person who has died. Joan's mother left trunks full of fine, tailored clothes, many of them handmade. Joan's mother was the same size as both Joan and Karen, the paid caregiver for the last two years of her life. When the clothes were being sorted, Joan offered Karen her choice, in appreciation for the good care her mother had enjoyed until her death. But Karen was horrified, saying she would never wear the clothes of any dead person, much less of someone she had loved. For Joan, wearing her mother's clothes was a loving remembrance of times when certain clothes had been worn, like birthdays and Thanksgivings.

Sometimes we are only dimly aware of the process by which we make our choices. Our jacket, coat, hat, purse, and shoes say a lot about our relationship to the community. We may dress differently to go to the store, bank, or dentist. Most of us tend to wear more formal clothes for a visit to a lawyer than to the hardware store. As we dress for an appointment, we make a hardly conscious estimate of the tastes of those we will see, and then we match them; we will be casual or formal, depending on the history of the relationship. The minutiae hidden in the act of choosing clothes for this or that task, act, day, or relationship tell us about our confidence or anxiety. Perhaps our choices will reveal a sense of competition or a wish to attract or impress; perhaps they will reveal an underlying lack of sense of self-worth or even an unconscious wish to undermine our conscious purposes.

Our clothes allow us to enact many different, often mutually exclusive personas. Jenny, for example, has a secret self that her current life-style suppresses almost entirely. She usually tends toward the comfortable, veering on sloppy, but she has another, preppy self who occasionally buys a silk blouse, lined wool slacks, or a blazer. These hang in her closet year after year. Sometimes she puts them on and admires the way she looks, but another part of her feels silly in them; she might get spots on them and need to have them cleaned. Back up they go, the inner, elegant persona unexpressed yet unrelinquished.

Ideally, we present ourselves in clothing in a manner that is both privately satisfying and socially flexible, a way that fits our life-style and sense of ourselves and can be used to respond to many different situations. But we may discover that we dress ourselves to express public selves that have either outlived their usefulness or are unnecessarily restricting. One sign of an identity in transition can be a pronounced worry about the appropriateness and acceptability of our clothing.

A few years ago, increasing arthritis in Susan's shoulder, wrists, and hands led to mounting frustration as she struggled daily with her Oxford button-down shirts and smartly tailored designer dresses. She felt increasingly trapped by these clothes, and one day she realized that a change to dolman sleeves would help solve her problem. Then she discovered pull-on elastic-waisted slacks. She began wearing her slightly less close-fitting clothes more often. A dressmaker put Velcro fastenings beneath buttons; she bought a new watch with a stretch band. It took several years to give up one image of herself as sleek and narrow for a bulkier look that maximized comfort and independence. She admitted to herself that the changes were final only when she was able to go through her closets and give away some of her most treasured tailored outfits.

For most of her adult life, Helen strongly favored muted blues and grays: her clothes, furniture, and cars were all somber, reflecting her self-image as a balanced, calm homemaker, the anchor for her colorful and lively family. But in time the children moved far away with their own families, her husband developed Alzheimer's disease, and her father died, leaving her depressed mother living alone nearby. Helen gradually began to feel dissatisfied with the lack of vibrancy in her life at home. After a critical look at her wardrobe, she indulged her secret wish to express the inner vividness she had suppressed for so many years. Clothes became a powerful symbol for her own need to go forward, to give voice to her own vibrancy in the face of her draining situation. She began by buying an aqua bathing suit, the first step in giving herself permission to take regular swims and hire a part-time caretaker for her husband. Her struggle with her guilt was a long one, with frequent qualms and anxiety about home as she swam laps. A maroon jacket and white summer dress, worn when she went out to meet friends, eventually followed the aqua bathing suit. Her increasingly bright wardrobe was a reflection of her gradual awareness that she was slowly and lovingly leaving her husband behind.

Sometimes the natural process of maturation, including changes in hair color and skin tone, body shape and musculature, will render obsolete our beliefs about what colors and styles look good on us. We may habitually buy dresses that emphasize what was once an unusually slender waist, wear low-cut blouses because we have always believed our necks to be among our best features, favor blue because we were always blond. We may cling obstinately to a young style, unwilling to confront who we are now, and risk looking absurd or pathetic. We have all noticed extreme examples of this: the elderly woman in teenage fashions makes us uneasy because she is betraying her intense wish to avoid being old. Letting go of ideas about what we look best in is a challenge, but the changes need not be seen as negative. Frances, for example, was slowly able to accept and take advantage of the changes in her body, discovering a dramatic new color range for herself when her hair went brilliantly white.

Now, as we too take a closer look at what we tell our worlds and ourselves as we dress, we may ask how nearly our public presentations match our private selves:

- Do we feel comfortable with our clothes, or are they masks that we are hiding behind, perhaps fearfully?

- Do they give us pleasure, or are they a strain?

- Is there rebellion in them, perhaps? Humor? Acquiescence to social norms?

- Are they part of a past that no longer serves our present?

Changes in our clothing and purse-carrying habits are easily accessible to all of us. The psychological cost to other members of our households is minimal, the changes can be made at our own pace, and they are fun. Furthermore, in this area the link between external and internal changes is particularly clear.

LIVING SPACES

Our next zone of safety is our living space. We stamp it with our own personalities; we feel safe within our arrangement of the objects that are most familiar to us.

First, we may ask if we have private space at all, or have we yielded our need for "a room of one's own" to the pressures and requirements of husbands, children, co-workers, friends, and pets?

If we have our own space, does it give us a sense of pleasure and control, and does it express ourselves as we are now? If not, what can be changed?

Ellen is a veterinary technician who until recently lived alone at the animal clinic rent free in exchange for night call duties. Then Ellen's elderly aunts, deaf and in failing health, asked her to come live in their small home and look after them. Out of a characteristic generosity and sense of duty, Ellen agreed. She was given the attic, which in her quiet way she transformed by painting it and having a larger window put in.

Ellen longed for a certain very expensive Swedish-made lounge chair. She would go into the store and sit on it and yearn, telling herself that she was thinking about scrimping and buying it for her aunts' living room. She believed that it was somehow too fine for her. But one day, in a burst of self-confidence soon after an operation that saved the life of a cat who had fallen from a window, she bought it and had it placed in her attic.

Now it is her throne, her nook, her private space in an otherwise chaotic and demanding house. She finds all her best thinking and reading is done there. The purchase also acted as a symbolic separation from her aunts, enabling her to come to a new level of detached kindness in her life with them. Her daring act has paid off handsomely on her inner balance sheet.

Few young mothers have space of their own; the extra space usually goes to children or to a husband's workroom or study. Mom's space, unless hard fought for, tends to be everywhere and therefore nowhere. If you have hungered for home space of your own, can creative thinking find you some? Even if it is basement or attic space, or a walled-off place in the porch or garage, fantasizing about your own space is the first step toward making it materialize. You may want to involve your family in a discussion of your need for privacy, not when you are feeling exasperated or trodden upon, but when moods are calm and the timing auspicious. It is always a good idea to share your plans and dreams with them in advance and anticipate their reactions.

Many women find themselves maintaining the children's rooms when the children begin to move away. Here is a potentially wonderful source of space that could be put to your use for a darkroom, a studio, a writing nook, or a place to stretch and exercise. However, even grown children may wish to sleep in "their" rooms when they come home to visit and can feel upset to discover that you have adapted their spaces to other purposes. You can always replace the bed with a fold-out couch, so that the child, or a guest, can continue to use the room as a bedroom when visiting. The children are growing and moving away; this is your recognition of that process. At the same time, as you create a new or different personal space, you create a metaphor for the new person emerging in you. Here are some questions to consider:

- How private are you about your home in relation to outsiders?

- Do you welcome friends and neighbors to drop in, or do you feel intruded upon?

- How do you feel about children or parents arriving unannounced?

- Can guests come into the bedroom?

- Are the doors of certain rooms in your home usually closed?

- Do you like to control the kitchen space, getting out the ice and serving guests drinks, or is it your style to wave them in the direction of the refrigerator with a "help yourself"?

- If it is safe to do so, is a key kept hidden outside for those in the know?

- If you aren't home, can your friends and relatives come in anyway?

As you think about the alternatives that describe you, become more aware of your sense of boundaries and how strict you are about them. If you are a committed boundary defender, it could be liberating to try, however briefly, to allow more openness in some area; if your boundaries are often breached and you are continually taken advantage of by others, defending your territory even in small ways could be a way of asserting a stronger sense of your needs.

This is also true in the realm of possessions. It is important to have some objects just for your own pleasure. How many times have we said, I must buy, get, alter, or paint this because of the children, spouse, parents, or friends? We can indulge ourselves a little and honor our needs as finances and energy allow. For some, the change may be a simple question of rearranging a room or giving away objects held on to for years, perhaps only because we thought someone else might want them. New objects bought simply for ourselves can be small: a reading lamp, a luxurious bath soap, or perhaps a coveted, finely designed skillet.

Whatever your particular home configuration, from the walled and moated castle to the crash pad that welcomes all comers, your challenge here is first to identify your pattern and then to experiment with expanding or contracting the borders in some way that you feel would produce valuable self-knowledge.

THE SELF ON WHEELS

The relationship to our car is often a very powerful, emotionally charged one. In part this is because it is an emblem of freedom and independence, a personal cocoon that allows us, within its safety, to leave the home nest behind while bringing some of it with us into the larger world.

Gail's well-intentioned parents assumed that after graduation their much-beloved only child would come home to live in Chicago. They gave her a gift of a good secondhand car that they expected she would use to drive back and forth between home and a job at her father's business. But Gail needed above all to avoid folding herself into a comfortable nest with her parents; she needed to be on her own, find her own job, rent a room, buy groceries, and pay taxes, all experiences that dorm life and family vacations had never given her. So, during a stormy afternoon, she outlined her plan to her parents: to drive west, explore until her small savings ran out, then work as a waitress or whatever else she could find. Her parents lost their child but found an adult that afternoon. Their gift had had unexpected consequences that forced them to let her go.

Many women discover that as they become increasingly self-confident their anxiety about their cars diminishes. Of course, levels of nervousness about cars can be dictated by practical as well as personal considerations: for a city dweller, an old wreck that she does not have to worry about on crime- and traffic-ridden streets could be an improvement over a sleek car needing a garage; for a confirmed nonmechanic, a late-model car and a good relationship with a maintenance shop may be worth the investment.

Think now about what your car tells you about how you imagine yourself. Your answers to the following questions may tell you about your level of intimacy with your car and about how anxious you are about mechanical reliability and safety in general:

- Do you feel proud or ashamed of your car?

- Do you wash, wax, and polish your car, or do you have others do it?

- If the inside of your car is untidy, is this because it is being well lived in or neglected?

- Do you ever look under the hood? What parts do you know the names of? What parts do you understand the function of?

- Do you know how to check your tire pressure? Oil level? Water level? Change a tire? Jump-start it? Do you want to know how?

- What are the security blanket items present or absent in your car: pressure gauge, healthy spare tire, jack, starter cables, maps, flashlight, rope, towing number, spare change, pencil, umbrella, first-aid kit?

For Alice, a high school teacher who lives half an hour from work, a reliable car that starts in frigid temperatures and downpours, one that hums along in harmony with her, is a crucial extension of her self. A small new click or buzz sends her anxiety level rocketing. No wonder new tires, frequent oil changes, and tire pressure checks are one of her highest budgeting priorities.

Molly, a horticulturist, has a far more relaxed attitude toward her ancient truck. It dribbles oil, and she patiently puts more in; it starts erratically, and she uses starter fluid; a tire has a slow leak, and she pumps it up regularly. She could buy another car, but the state of ill health of this one and the continuous inconveniences seem to bother her not at all. In fact, she finds real pleasure in her ability to keep the old wreck going, defying friendly advice and the car advertising industry.

As you think now about what your car and your relationship to it tell you about who you are now, imagine yourself the owner of another car very different in style, quality, and level of maintenance. If your car is not deeply a friend and you have been considering selling it or buying another, now is the time to take the first small steps: look at ads, visit dealers, talk to friends. Read *Consumer Reports*, consider your finances. Try out the idea, as prelude, perhaps, to eventually having the car you want.

Over the years Betty and her husband always owned practical vehicles: VW buses and station wagons for transporting the kids and their friends. Recently her husband left to remarry, taking the family car with him. Despite the equitable alimony, for the first few months Betty struggled with a poverty mentality; depressed and alone, contemplating but avoiding her transportation problem, she felt the junkiest old car would be no more than she deserved. But she had many supportive friends, and after the initial despair and self-recrimination had passed, she began to venture forth. She traveled a bit—one son is a pilot, so she has virtually free airfare—then took a writing course, courting disaster through overzealous dedication.

Coming out with a fine grade, she decided to reward herself by buying a new car. She knew what she admired most: a certain chic-looking, streamlined sports car. Her critical inner voice said, "You can't afford this. Where will the children sit?" And a second voice responded: "What children? They have cars of their own!" She went back and forth to the showroom four times until one of her sons, a newly minted lawyer, realized what was happening and wrote her a mock serious legal opinion that the car under discussion was the obvious choice. She bought her sports car, selecting a cheerful red, and discovered that her impulse had been right. Now she drives around like a queen, the car a constant reminder of her new self: mature, unattached, and smart.

Fay needed to move in the opposite direction. Her status-conscious husband had always selected one of a long line of expensive Buick sedans, and when she was divorced at thirty-one she decided to purchase a used Toyota. This was her statement about a new self and a declaration of independence from her marriage and the old values it implied. Practically, the Toyota was cheaper, easier to maintain, and smaller for city parking. But the car was also a reflection of her shifting concerns: the new Fay wanted to quit her highly paid advertising job to experiment with a career as a free-lance writer, scaling down her living standards and spending her money to satisfy her own needs, rather than the expectations of others.

Having a car that is yours alone means having space that is yours alone, with all the pleasures, freedoms, rights, and obligations that entails. Many women who once left the responsibilities for the car to fathers, boyfriends, and husbands are now learning about cars and mastering the skills and duties involved.

LUGGAGE

Like the car, the suitcase is a home away from home. We are not so different from hermit crabs, carrying our houses on our backs.

If we receive an invitation to go away for the weekend, we think instantly about the host's tastes and life-style, about the setting, the likely activities, and the weather. We also think about what persona to present:

- Proper, neat, and matching?

- Casual but elegant?

- Casual, with abandon?

For most of us, the clothes and objects we bring are not only practical necessities but also protections. They are security blankets against the anxiety of uncertain relationships with hosts or against our lack of confidence in skills like skiing, tennis, and socializing with other houseguests we may not know. We may fear that our physical endurance will not match what may be required. And then there is the dread of what is hardest of all for many of us: open, unstructured time. No wonder we often feel better if we bring along our knitting, crossword puzzle, or novel.

Some of us overpack, out of fear that we will need something and not have it, to the point that we have so much with us that it is impossible to find anything. Others are sparing to the point of foolishness and are caught with no sweater on a chilly evening at the beach, no suntan lotion on a hot day, no Band-Aids for blisters on a hiking trip, no change of clothes to wear to dinner when the hosts turn out to be more formal than expected.

Angela, a frequent visitor to areas of the Far East where gift giving is very important and foreign-made goods highly coveted, has a unique solution to the problem of how much to bring. She packs only things that she can both use and give away to her friends. Her aim is to maintain a balance in her suitcase while traveling, giving away her clothes gradually as she receives gifts. In this way she can wear a variety of clothes during the trip, and feel both prepared and free.

Next time you go on a short trip, conduct an experiment: change the size of the bag(s) which you pack. Overpackers may discover that by bringing only what they can fit into a small suitcase they feel pleasantly free—or they may find themselves in a panic, always looking for what is not there. Underpackers may find that they have a new sense of self-respect, knowing that they are prepared for more eventualities—or they may feel annoyed at having to lug around so much that is not essential.

Through such explorations, we may be able to increase our pleasure in our clothing, home arrangement, car, and patterns of packing; they may increasingly fit and accurately express our newly emerging selves. We may find that we will want to peel away unnecessary clutter, or that we will want to place more emphasis on acquiring fine things. We may decide that our old habits are best. No matter what the outcome, however, by trying new ways we will sharpen our appreciation of the process by which we shape our nests and boundaries. Through this new awareness, we will build nests that give us ever greater pleasure, comfort, and sense of who we are.

□

MINITASKS

In this series of exercises, you may want to pick tasks to consider your clothing, purse, and car, or you may want to concentrate on one area only.

1 ▪ Look at your closet and drawers objectively. Notice color ranges, texture preferences, clothes unworn for years (too small, too large, too fancy, too rugged, simply disliked). Write down on paper what you see: What selves are being brought along as baggage from the past? Note current selves that are missing or underrepresented: the jogger or partygoer, the newly sophisticated self, the public speaker, the woman who doesn't like to wear street clothes when she is at home alone. Note which colors and textures are working best for you as you are today. Think about directions you wish to pursue for the future.

2 • Ask a close friend to come over. Spread out makeup, hats, scarves, belts, skirts, slacks, tops. Together with the sense of freedom and fun of children, try new combinations, outrageous combinations, whatever roles or ideas come to you.

3 • Make a list of your best physical features:

a. as a child;

b. as a teenager;

c. as a young adult;

d. in middle age;

e. now.

Note the continuities, the additions and subtractions. Think about what clothing maximizes your best qualities today.

4 • Write a paragraph that describes your overall clothing style at each of the above stages. What cuts, colors, and fabrics did you favor? Again, note continuities and changes. If you discover that you are holding on to certain patterns out of habit, think about whether you wish to let them go.

5 • With a friend whose judgment you admire, go through your drawers and closet and take out *every* item needing

a. mending;

b. spot removal;

c. alterations;

d. ironing;

e. giving away;

f. throwing away.

Separate into piles and do it!

6 ▪ Borrow some jewelry that you feel is uncharacteristic of you. See how you feel wearing it. Lend your jewelry to someone else, and see whether this gives you a new perspective on you.

7 ▪ Consider your purse:

▪ How much do you care about how it looks?

▪ Do you have a series of purses and transfer their innards, or do you have one old steady?

▪ Does your purse add a finishing touch to an outfit?

▪ Is it actually a suitcase?

▪ Is it carried protectively close to you, or do you let it dangle?

▪ Is it held as an object of beauty, perhaps? Is it a shield, a weapon, or simply a container?

Now empty your most recently carried purse onto the bed and look hard, letting the contents tell you about your priorities, wishes, and fears. Change something: add, subtract, modify how it is organized.

If you use a hand purse, borrow or buy a shoulder bag and try it for one day, or vice versa.

8 ▪ Sit on your favorite chair: evaluate it for comfort, privacy, availability of light. Is there beauty or lack of it in what you can see from that position? If you are not satisfied, reorganize that space to maximize its function and pleasure for you. Find another light, surround yourself with favorite things, maybe even buy another chair. Involve those who live with you in what you are trying to do.

9 ▪ Draw a plan of your home or apartment as accurately as you can, from memory. Inside each room or space, make a list of

    a. functions;

    b. primary user(s).

Which are used most effectively, which least? Which are the pleasantest spaces, which the least? Which spaces do *you* use most, and for what? Rate each space on a scale of one to ten according to your satisfaction with the space and its use.

Now draw another plan of your home or apartment in which you change the proportions so that the size of the spaces in the house reflect their importance for you. If it turns out that for you, as it is for many women, the kitchen is enormous and the other spaces tiny, that may be a sign that you will want to carve out more space for yourself in some other area of your home.

10 ▪ Walk around your home. Find those objects, arrangements, pictures, and so forth that have become obsolete or simply obstacles. Rearrange the furniture in your favorite space, consulting and involving your co-habitants. Moving furniture can be a great game.

11 ▪ Look at the prints and pictures in your house. In one room, take them off the walls. Line them up and truly look. Remember how each arrived in your home and the memories and relationships that surround it. Put away or give away those no longer beautiful or important to you. Fix, reframe, and clean any of those needing care. Rehang the rest in places where you can see them freshly.

12 ▪ Empty the glove compartment and all pockets of your car. Fix, add, subtract: put the things back that you know you will need, that make you feel secure, that give you pleasure. Take away the junk. Check to make sure you have tools, jack, and flashlight.

13 ▪ With a knowledgeable friend, open the hood of your car and ask him or her to teach you just one thing, whether about function or maintenance.

14 ▪ When packing for a short trip, spread out in front of you everything you plan to take. Choose tops and bottoms so that several combinations are possible. If you are a minimalist, add some extras; if you overdo, be strict with yourself and see what happens. Do you feel uncomfortable at the thought of being without some solitary prop like a book? If so, try leaving it home and see what happens.

3 · Body Care

"You went through some changes there, Dr. Sacks,"
said one of them. "How about taking the first step
now?"

The first step! In my efforts to stand, to gain control,
I had thought only of holding on, of survival, of
standing, and not yet moving. Now, I thought, I might
try to move. . . . [The therapists] knew—priceless
knowledge, which the mind can forget—that there is
no substitute, ever, for *doing,* that "In the beginning
is the deed," and that there is no path to doing, no
way of doing, other than doing."

OLIVER SACKS

BOMBARDED WITH VARYING AND OFTEN CONTRADICTORY ADVICE
about what is good for us, we need to close the magazines and
figure out in a private place what we truly wish to change
about our own body care.

Which of the following statements do you agree with?

- I basically like my body.

- I am lazy about caring for my body.

- I need another person's approval to care about how
healthy I am and how I look.

- I have a nagging worry about my body that I am not dealing with.

- I am dealing ineffectively with a physical problem I know about.

We accuse ourselves of lack of discipline in relation to our bodies—as though "it" were separate from "me." We feel we *ought* to do things to it—make it jog, take sugar or calories away from it, stop putting nicotine into it. As we consider now how to change our relationship to our bodies, including how we feed ourselves, exercise, and seek health care, the very first step is to bring our bodies closer. We can join the "it" to the "me" by becoming more deeply responsible for our bodies, allowing ourselves pleasure because we like to live in them, not for what they convey to others, but for their own sakes.

This task becomes more urgent in adulthood, for the clock ticks more loudly and the more vulnerable systems in our bodies refuse to be ignored. They signal the need for new glasses, for a stricter avoidance of foods that give us indigestion, concessions to a knee that is undependable on stairs. At first it is easy to deny these warnings. Yet illness or pain can be the one friend that tells us truthfully that we must pay more attention.

Each of us has a unique vision of who we are beneath the skin. We are aware of carrying genes that predispose us to certain vulnerabilities: a spine that doesn't quite stack up as it should, a tendency to feel the cold because of poor circulation in the feet and hands, a family history of allergies, diabetes, or high blood pressure. Then there are the visual images of the body, fuzzy for most of us, from our school days: blood pressure, a ratio of numbers and a vague picture of liquids traveling under pressure through tubes; tangles of intestines absorbing food, to which different organs with various functions are joined; veins and arteries, colored red and blue as they were in our biology textbooks. We wonder if this mass of living matter is in good working order. Finally, we also carry memories and myths, often from our families, which have influenced our attitudes toward our bodies, loading them symbolically with connotations of strength, reliability, and health, or weakness, vulnerability, and disease. Family frailties often lie beneath the surface of our awareness in the form of latent threats. As we examine them, we may discover they are groundless or distorted—or quite real.

Anna, an advertising copywriter, was told during childhood that her father's siblings had both died in adolescence of epilepsy. Her father never spoke much about them; he had barely known them in his adult life, for he had run away and joined the navy, cutting off family connections. When Anna was grown, she told the epilepsy story to her fiancé, who became worried about their future children. Anna therefore contacted her father's much older sister, whom she had never met. She found her delightful. As they shared scrapbooks with each other, the sister told a very different story of the epilepsy deaths: true, they had had seizures, but these were the results of accidents, the sister's during a babyhood crib collapse and the brother's from the fall that eventually caused his death when he was a teenager.

Most families assign roles and characteristics to the various members, including physical descriptions. In many cases these are merely comparative: in an all-varsity family, the child who doesn't win trophies believes herself unathletic; in an obese family, the person of average weight is the skinny one; in a never-sick-a-day-in-my-life family, the one with a cold is an invalid. These notions from the past often lead to distorted ideas about our present capabilities and states of health.

From childhood Katie had a mild, chronic eczema in the crooks of her elbows and knees. She was treated as the sickly one, and finding a cure was a frequent subject of family conversation. The condition of Katie's skin became a barometer for family troubles of all kinds: whenever there was a crisis, there was renewed attention to Katie's health, and the eczema worsened as if on cue.

In college Katie entered therapy and gradually shed her self-image as frail and vulnerable. As many of us do, she chose a profession that helped her heal herself. Eventually she became a psychologist specializing in the connection between stress and dermatitis. As for her eczema, it's gone; she found that her problem was an allergy to wheat.

There are several levels of strategy in dealing with our body care:

a. prevention of illness and injury;

b. maintenance;

c. enhancement of health and strength;

d. dealing with symptoms of weaknesses as they appear;

e. coping actively with conditions that cannot be healed.

At whichever level we approach some small corner of wished-for change, we must attempt that single step with commitment and trust. No matter where we begin, whether it be in the area of weight and nutrition, exercise, or health care, change in one aspect will eventually infuse the other two, making us feel more looked after and respected by the most important source of such nurturance of all—ourselves.

WEIGHT AND NUTRITION

We look in the mirror and may not be pleased with what we see. Underlying our dissatisfaction with thighs, stomachs, breasts, or height is a beauty ideal: the "perfect" body, young, supple, and well proportioned. The dissatisfaction itself can be the enemy; health, vitality, and contentment add up to an attractiveness to which we as well as the world clearly respond.

Weight is many women's obsession. Although there is evidence for a genetic predisposition to obesity, most recent research favors cultural and familial factors. One sign is that overweight people often have overweight pets! In general, we have become an overweight, undernourished, flabby nation.

As children, some of us learned that to be good meant we would get a sweet treat; to be denied it was punishment. As adults, we drive to work, sit all day at desks, eat fast foods high in calories and low in nutrition, imbibe cup after cup of coffee and soda. The heavy meal is usually at the end of the day, when we least need energy from food; the relaxing drink adds more empty calories. Although we all know about the health hazards of coffee, alcohol, salt, saturated fats, and sugars, as a nation we are still heavy consumers of all of them.

Food is especially difficult for women. We are under tremendous pressure to maintain a slimness that is considered sexually attractive in our society, but at the same time we are expected to be the primary shoppers and preparers of food in our households. Eating, one of the most reliable and pervasive joys of life, has been perverted into a grotesque and frantic swing between indulgence and self-denial.

Our lives are established in a pattern of meals and snacks, preferences and dislikes. We skip breakfast or make a whole meal of it; we love vanilla and hate chocolate or vice versa; we never open a bag of chips without finishing the whole thing, or we can't stand junk food. Does your pattern satisfy you?

If not, what do you want to change: when you eat? what you eat? with whom you eat?

If you have one nutritional area that you would like to change, is it the habit of a lifetime?

Anthropologists have learned that cooking habits the world over are the last to change as people are influenced by outside cultures. If you feel stuck in your old patterns, it is little wonder. Perhaps the days of hamburger, bologna sandwiches, and SpaghettiOs are over if the little consumers are gone, taking their special tastes and quirks with them. But many of us retain some of our early routines.

It is especially rewarding to make changes in unsatisfying or unhealthy patterns around food. If we or someone in our household is on a special diet, such as one low in sodium or fat, new uses of herbs and spices and new methods of food preparation can make dealing with the challenge fun. We can stimulate our taste buds by shifting to steaming or wok cooking, or by using lemon, curry, or tarragon.

The first step is to identify your own patterns.

- Do you tend to broil, steam, fry, or bake?

- Do you rely on frozen foods or fresh?

- Do you enjoy lengthy preparation or is speed essential?

- How often do you use your spice rack?

- Which spices are left untouched year after year because you don't know much about their qualities?

- Which foreign foods are you curious about?

The means to expand our sense of taste are all around us, from TV's Julia Child and her offshoots to cooking classes and the Mexican, Chinese, and Indian foodstuffs that are now available in supermarkets.

Let us suppose that you want to cut down on your sugar intake for all the nutritional, caloric, and dental reasons you already know about. As part of your resolution to change, you have already moved from "ought to" to "want to"; and you are planning to start small. First, in your journal, detail for three days what you eat each day. Where does the sugar come in? Notice when you crave ice cream or cake: when you are tired? disappointed? pressured? Record what you feel. Writing this down locates where change is hardest and identifies the challenge. As you continue in this way to prepare to traverse this threshold, try to become very aware of sweetness in your mouth. Eventually you may find that you dislike too much of it.

An abrupt shift will probably register as deprivation, so using smaller amounts of sugar, perhaps simply placing a smaller spoon in the sugar bowl as a reminder, is one way to start. Try reaching for sweet fruit, such as raisins or oranges, instead of sugar. The people you live with will have to come up with their own commitment, so don't expect them to keep sweets out of the house. But they can encourage you, tease you a little, help you to stay with it. The appetite for something fades slowly but surely, and one day a candy bar may have lost its appeal.

The process of changing our nutritional habits thus involves commitment, a moderate approach, and the involvement of family or friends, whether our goal be more greens or less salt, more fluids or less fat. The specific item is less important than the attitude toward the enterprise. Yo-yo dieting, we know, doesn't work most of the time. A slow, self-respectful search for control will.

If we are within range of an acceptable weight, not dangerously obese or skinny, we would do well to think about our set points, the weight for which our bodies have a preference and to which they will usually return after periods of indulgence or dieting. If this level is a healthy one, we can work on letting go of unrealistic images and getting more enjoyment from food, our appearances, and our lives.

We often have trouble accepting that we periodically weigh more than usual, whether because of adolescent baby fat, giving birth, quitting smoking, being suddenly restricted to a more sedentary life-style, suffering an emotional upset, or simply indulging in too much good living. In fact, most of our faces look healthier when we are a little heavier; in winter a little more fat will keep us warm.

But we fear these changes because many of us unconsciously or consciously look to others, usually a man, to find us physically attractive, approve of us, and complete us. A good figure, sexiness, and love become equated in our minds. If we concentrate on living fulfilling lives on our own terms, with or without a partner as the situation warrants, this may help us stop eating with such guilt. The likelihood is that we will end up weighing more or less the same, whether or not we make ourselves suffer. We slowly gain a sense of pride in our figure, face, and way of moving as it is now and a sense of deep self-acceptance.

Dorothy is a tall woman with a regal presence cultivated during early training as a dancer. She shares a house with three other divorced women. They have in common both an occasional sense of missing something and a gentle delight in the new freedoms available to them now that they are without husbands. One of the many areas in which Dorothy has changed, under the influence of her housemates, is in her attitudes toward food.

As a young girl and woman struggling to become a professional dancer, Dorothy always battled food as something of an enemy. When a serious knee injury abruptly shattered her dreams, she went into mathematics, finding in the abstraction and logical proofs a sort of solace for her disappointment. The dancer image was burned deeply into her, however, and she habitually continued to deny herself desserts, gravies, dressings, and butter, maintaining her slim, lithe body well into her forties. Her husband, a fellow mathematician, was proud of her slenderness and was himself a fastidious eater.

After her divorce, Dorothy began to allow herself to take more pleasure in the preparation and consumption of food, the major evening social activity in her house of women. She discovered to her astonishment that she did not mind when she gained some weight. A series of prohibitions fell away: she began to look at ice cream as delicious rather than sinful, to see going out to a restaurant as a luxury rather than a trial of temptations. She looked forward to surprising her housemates with special dishes and became known as the in-house specialist in salads and exotic casseroles.

Impossible cultural ideals and imagining a critical audience can tyrannize us into self-hatred. Preoccupation with weight brings pleasurelessness in food, hopelessness or desperation about exercise, and ultimately self-rejection. But although it can be difficult, we do have the option to reject these values, as Dorothy did, in favor of those that emphasize good health and the beauty within.

EXERCISE

The discovery of the joys of exercise can be one of the positive outcomes of illness. At forty-two, having raised five daughters, Shirley had little interest in exercise; her serious hobby was weaving, and she loved going to sheep fairs to look for fine wool, carding and dyeing it and making it into shawls, which she would sell at craft shows. Never financially profitable, her craft was a source of deep satisfaction, and she never felt any need to spend her spare time in any other way.

Then, after a routine checkup, her doctor ordered a mammogram and a malignancy was discovered. Shirley would need a total mastectomy. A month of anguish followed, in which Shirley rewrote her will and talked pessimistically with her husband and daughters about the future.

Surgery went well, but the recovery was long; Shirley had come into the hospital somewhat heavy and out of shape. Doctors recommended diet and exercise. Frightened into preventive action, Shirley began a discipline of long daily walks. Her husband, anxious and concerned, joined her. Their walks gradually became habit and then a pleasure not to be missed; she and her husband rediscovered a sense of companionship that had been dormant in the marriage for many years.

As she began to feel stronger, Shirley began experimenting with jogging. She found she liked the sweaty, panting high, the cleansing shower and sense of well-being she always had after a run. Her husband, once again supportive, read up on the physiology of running. Slowly they became a team, she the athlete and he the coach. He loved monitoring her distances, timing her heartbeat, helping her with her diet; he too ate differently and lost weight.

What began as a life-saving mandate to exercise grew gradually into a passion. Now Shirley is a long-distance runner who completes races with the best in her age group, and her husband is the keeper of the records, trophies, and photo album, the water carrier cheering from the sidelines.

Most of us admire friends who swim, jog, or go to yoga class regularly. Many of them have carried into their adult lives an active enjoyment of physical activity. For these committed exercisers, adulthood has meant only adaptation: less frequent tennis games, fewer laps in the pool. But most of us lose the habit when we have children or our careers become intense. During those pressured years, exercise is likely to be the first activity, along with reading for enjoyment and time alone, to be sacrificed. With little experience or taste for physical activity, we have to find the discipline to start again.

An inner debate begins. "But everybody else in aerobics class is very young and fit, and they'd only laugh at me." Or "I don't know anyone else who plays squash. I don't even know where my racket is." And "I would look silly in jogging shorts."

As we all know, it is never too late. Louisa, a diabetic amputee of eighty, now exercises from her wheelchair for half an hour a day. Her spine, shoulders, neck, arms, fingers, and facial muscles get an intensive workout. Because she loves the warm afterglow, and because she is determined to be as strong as she possibly can despite her handicaps, she is able to do this entirely through her own self-discipline, using cassette tapes, without a teacher, partner, or group. But this is precisely where many of us need help. We cannot seem to find the stimulus to exercise by ourselves.

We can begin by remembering some period of pleasurable physicality from childhood or adolescence. Forget the negative comparisons with your high-energy, high-performance friends. At whatever level you practiced, what was the nature of the enjoyment for you?

49

- Was it the companionship and spirit of being part of a team, as in volleyball?

- Was it the thrill of winning, whether in competition against yourself, as in handicapped golf, or over an opponent, as in tennis?

- Did you love the meditative, energetic flow of a long swim?

- The crystalline zest of skiing?

- The long, lyrical stretch and strength of yoga?

- The pleasure of becoming more competent under the guidance of a beloved teacher, as in figure skating?

- The dressing room gossip before and after exercise class?

- The clubby sociability around the bowling team?

- Did you take pleasure in the sweat, or was the reward in the aftereffects, in your pride in knowing you looked healthier and felt more comfortable when you were in shape?

This backward look cannot, perhaps, restore to you the exact activity you loved. But you can find some form of exercise that gives you a similar delight. If you know you need a team, find a team; if you know the relationship to a teacher is crucial, begin the search with that in mind.

Suppose you have always loved to go dancing. Just moving to music was a liberating pleasure; in college, your waltz and tango were a sensation. You didn't marry that fellow dancer, though, you married someone you loved more, someone who had everything, including two left feet. Dancing fell out of your life because it never seemed appropriate for you to go dancing without him. Now you remember how much fun you used to have. "But a woman can't go out dancing alone!" you say. Perhaps not, but there are other ways to get started again. There might be a ballroom dance class in your community center. You feel shy? Never mind, take a woman friend with you or just go. A folk-dancing group or an exercise class might be another possibility; for you, the key is to find a way of combining movement and music.

Perhaps you were once an accomplished figure skater or ballet dancer. Some find it painful to return to an activity that they once did well. They stop entirely rather than insult what they loved by a performance that is less than their best. Yet this is denying possible pleasure. If you are among these retired artists and athletes, perhaps you would be happier with something related to but not identical to the area in which you once excelled: substitute aerobics or yoga for ballet, cross-country skiing for downhill racing, badminton for volleyball.

Perhaps as a girl you always loved swimming. The ocean was a natural habitat when you were growing up on the coast. As a young woman you moved inland, and now you remember your connection with the sea. You think about swimming, but you live in Iowa. True, swimming pools are not what you were used to, but they do hold water. Most cities and towns have pools in health clubs, hotels, or universities. Give it a try, taking a friend who likes to swim; enjoyment often doubles with good company. Or, during the summer, try the local swimming hole or state park. You may surprise yourself and recapture some of that early delight. But start small. Don't buy an expensive membership in an exercise club until after you've tried it out, or you may frighten yourself off by overambitiousness. On the other hand, paying the membership fee may make you feel that you will stick with it long enough to get over your ambivalence.

Even in its mildest forms, physical training has an inevitable component of pleasure as you become stronger and more competent, watch your gains in endurance or flexibility week by week. Exercise grows into a habit quickly, especially if others are involved. Soon you will find yourself unable to say to yourself, "Not today." If you begin slowly, ten minutes a day, once a week or every day in structured form, it can even become a passionate commitment, as we know from some of our jogging, golfing, and tennis-playing acquaintances who absolutely cannot stop.

HEALTH CARE

We are beginning to take more responsibility for what we allow to be done to our bodies. The morass of conflicting medical advice leads us now more frequently toward second opinions, refusal of treatments, and investigation of alternatives. We are realizing that just because we have gone to one doctor for ten years is no reason not to look elsewhere; we can always meet a new doctor without committing ourselves to his or her care. Some women have found that alternative forms of healing such as acupuncture and acupressure, osteopathy, rolfing, vitamin and nutrition therapy, massage, and so on have been important supplements for more traditional methods or have helped them where traditional medicine could not. Many of us have now established the habit of taking vitamins and drinking plenty of water as preventive measures.

Here are the stories of three women who passed through thresholds of change with their own medical situations:

Living alone with her two teenage sons in her farmhouse in Connecticut, thirty-eight-year-old Nora is a market gardener who supplies local restaurants with fine vegetables. She is used to being outdoors and active in all weather. Three years ago, however, arthritis of her neck and upper back began to cause frequent, immobilizing spasms of pain.

Her doctor took X-rays and found that the buildup of calcium in the vertebrae was considerable; he told her that although she could take as much Tylenol as she liked, her condition would not improve and there was little he could do for her. Angry with the medical profession and with her body for having betrayed her, especially at so young an age, Nora refused to accept his judgment. She discovered that hot baths seemed to soothe her; Jacuzzi treatments felt even better. She began to read about the connections between arthritis and diet and changed her eating habits. She found a masseuse who helped her locate the neck muscles that were locked, and slowly they worked on releasing them. A chiropractor adjusted her lower back, which had been affected by the problems with her neck. Then Nora found Feldenkrais, an alignment therapy that repatterns movement so that muscles and nerves can take new pathways. Two years after the first panic, Nora could move again with only minor constraints and was more calmly accepting of the spasms when they came.

Beatrice was diagnosed as having the early symptoms of osteoporosis in her hip joints. She was advised to increase calcium intake through more green vegetables, nuts, and dairy products and to take up an exercise with impact, which increases bone density. Although Beatrice had never been athletic, even as a child, and was unwilling to exert herself and afraid of challenges, her memory of her bedridden grandmother, who was always falling and breaking bones, drove her to take short jogs every afternoon before dinner. She was amazed, after a week of painful exertion, stiffness, and continuous doubt, to discover that she began to look forward to the exhausted but stimulated feeling that came at the end of her run. She now feels optimistic that her efforts will strengthen her bones.

Of the two women, Nora let go of accepted authority figures and treatments; Beatrice adopted an exercise habit that was foreign to her. Driven by their own discomfort, they had to overcome their initial resistance and take risks. The solutions each found may not be for everyone; we all have patterns that predispose us to reject or respond to certain types of treatment. But we can learn from Nora's and Beatrice's willingness to try new things. The key is flexibility, openness, and determination. Taking charge also means accepting and adapting to the levels of pain and deterioration that are unavoidable.

Solving physical problems may also require working through

deep emotional issues that may be contributing to the symptoms. Jean, for example, is the affluent thirty-seven-year-old wife of a realtor. She plays tennis in her spare time, but there hasn't been much of that; among her many volunteer responsibilities, she is on the boards of a large foundling hospital and of the city's symphony orchestra.

Her physical troubles began during a tennis tournament. Suddenly her shoulder, elbow, and wrist froze, and she could not move them at all. Doctors offered many diagnoses: arthritis, tendonitis, muscle tension. Jean tried cortisone, ultrasound, pain relievers—nothing seemed to work. In despair, she turned to a physical therapist, with whose help the intense pain subsided. Jean began to explore the deeper sources of tension. As she discussed her frustration with the fact that her speed and accuracy seemed to be diminishing, she became aware of some of the rage underlying her tennis game.

Then one day there was a breakthrough: as the therapist worked on her shoulder, Jean felt an overwhelming urge to hit out. This reminded her of the terrible fights she used to have with her two brothers, who would dare her to wrestle, then gang up to subdue her, pin her down, and laugh. She burst into tears. With the therapist's help, she realized that the frozen shoulder held her rage; her choice of sport had been her way of hitting back. Months of emotional exercises in pillow-punching followed. The shoulder became increasingly mobile. When the therapy was completed, Jean was not only wiser, but able to return to tennis, now a more joyful game.

Jean was lucky; she found the right person to work with. Think now about whom are you working with toward your healthiest self:

• Do you respect, like, and feel comfortable with your family practitioner, internist, gynecologist, dermatologist, dentist, chiropractor, oculist, and/or masseuse?

- Are you putting off an exam in some area of preventive care? If so, which of the following is your excuse?

  a. I am not concerned enough.

  b. It is too expensive.

  c. It would be painful.

  d. It would be embarrassing.

  e. I don't have time.

  f. My insurance doesn't cover it.

  g. I am uncomfortable with the health care professional.

  h. I haven't got a health care professional for this problem.

Postponing care, whether it be an eye exam, mammogram, blood pressure or cholesterol reading, dental cleaning, X-rays, or follow-up care, can be dangerous. Perhaps you dislike the practitioner or just hate the waiting room. You may have vague symptoms that suggest a possible problem, and you'd rather not have your fears confirmed. If so, such early warnings are trying to signal you, to buy you time.

Lucy's mother developed a mark on her thigh when she was in her mid-forties. Although the mark grew every year, she never showed it to a doctor, perhaps because she tended to put the needs of her family before her own, perhaps because she was unable to deal with her fears. When the growth became enormous, even her adult children noticed it and began to pressure her. When she finally had it looked at, it was too late: the malignancy could not be controlled, and she was dead within the year. Lucy and her sister harbor a deep anger at their mother for not taking care of herself better, and they blame their father for his failure to notice what must have been obvious for many years.

Stories of this kind, so familiar, are sobering messages. Yet it is neither our partner's nor our children's responsibility to see that we value and care for our bodies. Only we can look critically at our current habits of care and the underlying attitude toward our bodies, then become better informed by reading and listening.

As we decide now to commit ourselves to one small challenge, whether in eating habits, fitness, or health care, we can take heart in the knowledge that it may eventually influence other areas. A commitment to exercise may radiate into attention to skin care and hair care and in turn into cutting down on sugar or alcohol. Our body is the only one we have, and our care for it, no matter where we begin and in how small a way, is a deep mark of respect for it and for our selves.

☐

MINITASKS

Again, you should feel free to choose tasks from all sections or only one or two of the areas covered in this series of minitasks.

1 ▪ As you answer the following questions about your family patterns of food consumption, physical energy, and health, consider how closely the patterns of your childhood family match those of the same people now. Then compare them with those of yourself and your new family (if you have one) today. Your answers should reveal much about how you have or have not changed in the area of body care over the years. They should also tell you how much you have adopted from past family attitudes and tendencies—and indicate areas that you may now wish to reconsider and change.

Body Care

a. Weight and Nutrition

- As a group, how aware of nutrition was your family during your childhood?

- What about your parents and siblings today?

- What about you and your family today?

- On the whole, was your family overweight, underweight, or average?

- What about today?

- What about you and your new family?

- What were some of the family eating patterns then?

- Are there changes today?

- What about you and your new family?

b. Exercise

- Find three different-colored pens. With the first, circle the adjectives that describe your family physically, during your childhood:

outdoorsy   energetic   well-coordinated   athletic

competitive   hyperactive   sedentary   clumsy   lazy

- What about now? (Use another color.)

- What about your new family group? (Use the third color.)

- When you were young, were there family members whose physical ability was outstanding in some area?

- How able were you in comparison with them?

- What about now?

- Were there those much weaker or out of shape?

- What about now?

c. Health Care

- Do you believe your childhood family to have been generally healthy or sickly?

- What about now?

- What about your new family?

- What is the longevity pattern of your family: are they generally long-lived into a peaceful old age? hard-living, with an early burnout?

- To what diseases is your family genetically predisposed?

- Did your childhood family put a lot of energy into medical care, or did they tend to neglect themselves?

- What about now?

- What about you and your new family?

2 · Consider now the physical role assigned to you in the family when you were a child:

- Were you the sickly one?
- The athlete?
- The picky eater?
- The family fatty?
- The family beauty?
- The hypochondriac?

- How would you describe yourself now in relation to them?

- Is your role in your new family the same or different?

Weight and Nutrition

3 • To evaluate your eating habits, list the five most healthy habits you have. Then list the unhealthy ones. Which unhealthy one would be easiest to change? Start with that. Eliminate that habit for two weeks, then consider whether you wish to continue.

4 • Put a glass at your bathroom sink. For three days, drink a glass of water every time you urinate, even if you are not thirsty. Try to develop this into a habit.

5 • Chart your weight set point by drawing a graph of your approximate weight over the past ten years. If it has been more than ten years since you have been at what you think is your ideal weight, try to let go of that as your ideal. Set points do change over the course of our lives.

6 • With a friend, go through all the canned and dry foods in your kitchen. Weed out anything that you have not used for two years.

Trace how each of these foods arrived in your kitchen. Was it a gift, an item you bought in response to what you thought someone might like, an exotic impulse that seemed too unfamiliar to use? Give them all away, keeping only those foods that continue to intrigue you. Use one of them in the next meal you prepare.

7 • Sort your herbs and spices into three groups: those never used, those so seldom used they are more than two years old, and those used frequently. Get rid of those in the first group, unless one or two pique your curiosity. Read in a cookbook about using them. Throw out everything more than two years old; replace those you use occasionally. Label and date the new ones. Take a pinch of each and rub it between your fingers; with closed eyes, memorize the fresh smell.

Exercise

8 · Lie on the floor with your knees bent up and your spine straight. Close your eyes and relax completely. Very slowly, mentally travel up your body, sensing your toes, ankles, calves, knees, thighs, hips, lower back, stomach, waist, ribs, chest, shoulders, arms, wrists, hands, neck, and head. Are there muscles that hurt? Are there parts that feel sore or tight? Focus your concentration and breath on those parts and see if you can help them relax.

What parts of your body seemed tight, blocked, or painful? Write them down, then find exercises, or help, for problem areas.

9 · For those who used to exercise but have fallen out of the habit: Make a list of several physical activities that you have liked in the past. Rate them in terms of the enjoyment you took in them and the level of skill you attained. Then answer the following questions about these activities:

- Were they team or individual?

- Were they part of structured classes or things you did as the mood took you?

- Were equipment and/or special space required?

- Were there other elements beyond the actual activity that contributed to the experience (music, a feeling for a teacher, social life)?

10 • Consider what your current situation suggests, in the light of your answers. If, for example, the music and friendships of a childhood ballet class were important to you, but you now feel classical ballet would be too strenuous, try a folk-dance class. If you loved field hockey, investigate team sports at your local community center. If you were always an individualist, a runner, skier, or gymnast, but have given up your sports habit, consider making a compact with a friend to run or jog-walk. Report to yourself in your journal.

11 • For the committed nonexerciser: Make a list of every physical activity available in your area. Cross off those that are absolutely out of the question for you, in order of abhorrence. Don't permit yourself to cross off the last one: try it, just once. Even a TV exercise class could count. Give yourself a gold star for willingness, even if you end up hating it!

12 • For those who don't know what activity is right for them: Make a list of friends and acquaintances in your age group. Talk to each of them about what physical exercise has meant to them in their lives. Write down what, if anything, they do and how often. Ask them if you can go with them once, if they will help you get started, even if it means being in a different-level class or spending less time. Go with a different friend each week. After you have tried several activities, see what you have enjoyed most and would like to return to.

Health Care

13 • Make a list of your doctors, dentist, and other health care professionals. Rate them on the graph below on a scale of one to ten according to your estimate of professional competence and capacity to listen and help you clarify your concerns.

	Competence	Capacity to Listen	Ability to Clarify	Total Score
General Practitioner				
Internist				
Gynecologist				
Dermatologist				
Obstetrician				
Dentist				
Chiropractor				
Eye Doctor				
Therapist/Counselor				
Masseuse				
Others				

Those with marks below six, in any category, need to be seriously reassessed. Ask friends or professionals in whom you have confidence for other recommendations.

14 ▪ Lay out a written plan for six months of preventive health care for a well-loved best friend of an age and state of health similar to your own. Now consider it a plan for yourself. Is there anything you have prescribed for her that you would be unlikely to follow through on for yourself? Is there something you are afraid of?

15 ▪ If you are putting off health care, itemize your worst fears and fantasies. Find a friend who is also avoiding preventive health actions and make a pact to spur each other into making (and keeping) appointments.

4 · Money

Who is rich? He who rejoiceth in his portion.

THE TALMUD

DONNA, A DEVOUT METHODIST FROM A WORKING-CLASS FAMILY, IS an ambitious, self-made woman. When she was in her teens, her domineering mother told her that there were two ways for a woman to leave home: die or get married. Soon after, Donna married her first suitor, an agreeable and handsome neighborhood swain whom she knew hardly at all.

At thirty Donna found herself with four children and a mostly unemployed, semialcoholic husband. Forced into the role of head of family, Donna took a job at a securities brokerage. Thanks to her good head for figures and sharp business sense, she soon rose to the position of assistant manager. At the same time, with a small amount of capital, she began to buy and sell stocks.

Her husband was useless around money; when he had it, he practically gave it away. So Donna handled all the financial decisions. She liked it, and he seemed content to allow her to take charge.

What seemed to be a livable compromise with her husband proved a fatal mistake in dealing with her children. Donna expected them to let her handle their money, too, and to contribute to the cost of living. As soon as her eldest son had his first paper route, at twelve, she taxed him.

And so the endless fights over money began. Donna never felt she was doing anything but teaching her children the responsibilities of money. They felt as if she were a queen bee, they her worker bees, and that she had given birth to them only to increase the strength of the hive. In their view, no one seemed to taste the honey but she.

Donna became increasingly skillful at investing, unerringly sensing the undervalued stock, diversifying into real estate and gold, knowing exactly when to put something on the market and how to wait for the best price. She loved the sport of managing her portfolio, seeing herself as building her family's financial strength. Her passion for money management grew so strong that even personal and emotional decisions were based on whether or not they were financially sound.

Her children were asked to contribute their savings to these ventures. They did so, out of a complicated sense of guilt and obligation. Sometimes they got their money back, sometimes not. Donna would tell them that someday they would inherit these projects—the ski resort condo, the old house they spent so many hours renovating—but her ventures were always sold, at a profit that was quickly reinvested in her name, and the dreams vanished.

Today, Donna's control of money is her way of ensuring her family's involvement with her and each other; even as adults, her children have never lived farther than a few miles away, moving back home in times of personal crisis. Donna's husband leaves her periodically but always comes back. They are all caught in a web of interdependency, habit, and guilt. In this delicate dance choreographed by Donna out of her need for security and power, she is rich in actual financial terms, but needy beyond what money can buy.

For all of us, as for Donna, the twisted rope of money has two strands. The first is mythic, emotional, and value-laden, created by our early histories and strengthened by our subsequent experiences with money and its uses; the second is the practical strand that is the actual inflow and outflow of income and expenditures. In exploring our emotional attitudes toward money, the practical aspects of our use of money will become clearer; as we become more capable in practical financial matters, our level of anxiety decreases. Our goal here is to explore our boundaries and habits, to lower the level of anxiety or pleasurelessness in money, and to more nearly achieve a balance and harmony between our inner desires and our practical needs. Think now about the thresholds that you might wish to traverse, both in the way you feel about money and in the way you actually handle it.

MONEY AND FAMILY HISTORY

Our relationships with money are rarely consistent, whether over the course of our lifetimes or between our inner and outer lives. We may have had a poor childhood and be wildly spendthrift in adulthood or vice versa. We can feel rich without a dime or poor with millions of dimes.

Nancy's mother came from a well-to-do family that lost most of its estate when Nancy was a young teenager. The messages about money that Nancy was given as she grew up were bafflingly mixed. There were expensive party dresses and English wool coats for church and visits; the rest of the time there were pinching shoes and old clothes mended and re-hemmed for the third time. There was a deep sense of shame about the family's poverty and valiant attempts to conceal it. The fine linen, silver, antiques, and other accoutrements of old wealth that remained were covertly prized. Nancy learned that it was admirable to make do with very little and that conspicuous consumption should be despised.

In the course of renovating the family home for sale, Nancy

developed skills like painting, carpentry, and tiling. Beginning informally, Nancy then began to work on neighbors' homes as a way of earning money for school. These skills became her profession: she now runs a small home repair business. She earns a comfortable income, but she lives in old work clothes and drives a rattly truck. However, next to her skin she wears the finest silk underwear, and she still polishes and uses the family silver, one of the only vestiges of her heritage.

Consider now your early memories of money, your family's attitudes, and your actual financial situation:

- What did money mean to you in your childhood?

- Was there a sense of plenty or a sense of poverty?

- Were family finances discussed?

- As a teenager, did you have an allowance or bank account?

- How old were you when you earned your first wages?

- Did you learn how the stock market worked and what insurance was, or was money hidden and mysterious?

- Did you learn enough about money to be prepared to handle your own finances?

- Did your parents ever quarrel about money?

Money may have been used in our families in subtle and sometimes destructive ways, to control, to manipulate, to withhold, to bribe for acquiescence or love. Money, a powerful metaphor for self-worth, may also have been treated as a measuring stick for success.

Serena never had to worry about money when she was growing up. Her parents did not expect her to work her way through college; they paid for her education, wanting her to have the opportunities that as immigrants they themselves never had. Even after college, when Serena explored becoming a professional modern dancer, they were eager to help her. Despite this comfortable parental cushion, however, Serena felt like a waif, rarely buying anything for herself or indulging herself in a treat.

Returning to graduate school in dance therapy, Serena won a series of fellowships that seemed to her to be, like her parents' money, income that she had not really earned. She continued to shop only in used-clothing stores and to eat her spartan, vegetarian diet. Unlike the other graduate students who complained that the $5,000 stipends left them broke, Serena always had plenty in the bank.

Later, when she married and began earning a respectable income as a personal fitness trainer, she put her funds in conservative bank certificates of deposit, where she ignored them. Even with several thousand dollars in savings, she felt financially insecure. Salespeople in fashionable clothing stores intimidated her: these shops seemed not to be intended for her. Her "stinginess," and conflicts over money, were a major cause of her divorce.

Beginning to see her odd relationship to money as a serious problem, Serena understood that she was indeed ungenerous, especially toward herself. She told herself that this was because, as a free-lancer, she never felt sure of her ability to earn a living. She knew, too, that growing up in the 1960s had instilled in her a deep reluctance to "consume." But what she could acknowledge only in part was that her parents were often manipulative of the contract implied in their giving, expecting from her a gratitude and indebtedness that made her uncomfortable about accepting their money and even more reluctant to spend it. This had colored all her use of money with guilt. She felt worthless, as if she did not deserve the things that money could buy. Even now, in her forties and remarried to a wealthy attorney, with a bank account of her own, Serena drives a $175 Chevy, clips coupons, and never sets foot inside a boutique. Within herself, she is still a waif.

MONEY AND OUR INNER LIVES

As with Nancy and Serena, our use of money is often extremely complex and holds a mirror to our characters. It sen-
sitively reflects our attitudes toward giving and receiving, power
and dependency, and our concern with the future.

Some people need the support and permission of others to
spend money on themselves. Priscilla runs a small dairy farm
with her husband and teenage son. For much of her adult life,
the family was committed to reinvesting profits in equipment
and animals, so although they were doing well, there never
seemed to be much to spend on extras. In their late forties, however, they decided that the operation should grow no larger, and
they resolved to take things more slowly and enjoy life.

For years Priscilla had followed the career of Andrew
Wyeth, buying postcards and reprints of his work wherever she
found them. Then a beautiful retrospective volume was published. Although Priscilla could not stop thinking about it, the
staggering price tag made it seem out of reach. She told herself
that the neighbors would think her ostentatious if she bought
it, and that the money should go to something everyone in the
family could enjoy. In the midst of this private battle, her
husband showed her a newspaper ad for the book. His enthusiasm made Priscilla rethink her "selfishness." After three trips
to the bookstore, she exuberantly brought it home.

We too may have noticed the need for permission to spend
on ourselves: shopping with an encouraging friend or receiving
a gift certificate gives us the impetus to buy with less guilt.

Some prepare for the future by saving. Saving implies an
expectation of life ahead; it is also a protection against catastrophe. Security against the unknown, inflation, education
expenses, or job loss impel us to save or to feel as if we ought
to. Others feel less of a need to save, whether out of confidence
in their ability to bring in future income, a belief in life as a
short-wicked candle, or perhaps a self-destructive unwilling-
ness to contemplate a time when they will be old.

- Do you generally tend to fear impoverishment or trust a benevolent future?

- Do you have a pattern of spending everything quickly?

- Do you hoard your money in some form?

- Are you a spender who wishes she could be a hoarder?

- Are you a hoarder who wishes she could be a spender?

- Are you overly tight, given your actual situation?

- Are you overly generous?

- If you have ever purchased a CD or an IRA, how did it make you feel? Clever? Secure? Poorer than before? Richer?

For Helen, a free-lance computer consultant who usually makes about $17,000 a year, money is like a river flowing through her life. It has an intangible quality; it either appears or doesn't, and then it flows out from her to others just as easily. This, she can see, is obscurely related to an unwillingness to have to lock her house or car and to a need to be able to give away any book, necklace, or blouse if someone truly admires it. There is an easy circularity that her friends notice. Her checkbook is only vaguely balanced; there isn't much left at the end of each month. Helen trusts the future.

Her friend Stella, who teaches mathematics in junior high school, couldn't be more different. She puts a star on pay day in her calendar; she writes checks with the fear that she may have overspent. This has never happened, since she computes all of her expenses. Although only thirty-two, she visualizes her old age as a downward spiral into illness and poverty. She enters contests and lotteries, clips discount vouchers, and follows the interest rates in different banks and moves her funds accordingly. She uses the ATM machines to check her balance almost every day, out of a need for reaffirmation that there is plenty. She once found a $42 bank error, and she enjoys telling people about it. The bank is an adversary to be treated with caution and bested whenever possible. In a recurrent nightmare, she goes to the teller's window to get a balance, and the teller has no record of her name or account.

Helen and Stella are both unusual, one living for today without a thought for the future, the other hoarding and hedging against a multitude of possible catastrophes and terrors. Most of us have a more moderate need for security.

MORE THAN ENOUGH

What do you usually do when you have more money than you need for basic survival?

Having more money can free us to buy things, give to others, and enjoy life more. The arrival of the bills is no longer bad news; it no longer matters whether the bills or the paycheck arrive first.

Shelley is one example of someone who learned to appreciate money after doing without. Living on a fixed salary, she at last finished building her little house after five years of scrimping. Each self-denial equaled a faucet or a window screen or electric outlet. When the big things were all paid for, Shelley began to have a little extra each month, which she used to buy new towels and upgrade her telephone. Then came the day she bought herself a new nightgown: this was the first luxury she had bought not for the house but for herself in five years. It seemed unbelievably dear to her.

Although those years were very hard for Shelley, she feels she would do it all over again the same way. Furthermore, not having enough for a time made money a consciously appreciated gift that she will never again take for granted.

Wealth, especially suddenly acquired by legacy or windfall, can have its pitfalls. It requires an immediate and shocking readjustment not only of actual life-style, but of our social networks as well. There may be a move to a more comfortable home, subtle shifts in power relationships with friends, lovers, or children. Suicide is not uncommon among million-dollar lottery winners.

Tina has spent her way through two large fortunes. The first was the two-million-dollar inheritance that she received when she was twenty-one; the second came in late middle age, when her lover died and she was left another four million.

The first fortune lasted less than five years. It leaked away into the hands of this one who needed a car, that one with a gambling debt, the other one who wanted to begin a business. People swarmed about, but when the money was gone, so were they. With the habit of largesse and elegance dying only gradually, Tina continued to convey an aura of gracious plenty, her classic cashmere and fur coats and fine handbags lasting years.

At thirty-five she settled down with an affluent lover, and her style once again approximated the reality. When he died twenty years later, she was his sole heir. Once again the well-wishers arrived to enjoy the free flowing of money, but the semblance of friendship lasted only as long as the funds did.

Tina is now near eighty, vague and puzzled by life, slowly selling off the remaining pictures and fine jewelry. She is alone and will soon be destitute.

Affluence can impose another kind of burden: if there is no need to work, we can quickly lose our sense of self-worth and purpose. Those of us who have a strain of reclusiveness may even have to live with the curse of never needing to leave the house.

At thirty-seven Eleanor became the sole heir to her father's estate. Single, she had worked in New York City all her adult life as copy editor for a major publishing house. Where to work, what rent to pay, how to conserve and spend, had been ongoing questions of survival. But after the thousandth book on a less-than-fascinating subject, she felt burned out and tired of city living. Lovers came briefly into her life, but she found that the effort to find one who was eligible and compatible was exhausting.

Her inheritance represented an escape: suddenly the issue of making the money to live vanished. She joyfully gave notice at work. But to her surprise, after the first spending spree she lost interest in buying the things she had imagined for herself and seemed unable to gather the energy to find a new place to live. She sat in her dingy basement apartment, each day a void filled with nibbling, television, and sleep. She now had money without pleasure and time without use.

After some months of relative seclusion, Eleanor became aware of her need for filled time, which she had once confused with the burden of making money. She volunteered to edit pamphlets for the art museum up the street, assigning herself responsibilities as binding as those she once had at work. She is now no happier than she was before her inheritance, but at least she is busy again. The management of her investments has become an enjoyable game, but Eleanor also understands that money for her is a dangerous friend that can trap her into immobility.

MONEY AND FRIENDS

We all use money in a wide range of symbolic areas in direct and indirect communication with the others in our lives. Even at the simplest level, any two people, whether lovers or friends, act and react to each other around money.

Most of us have probably known people whose need to keep accounts to the last nickel has spoiled a friendship and others who are so generous that they seem to bring out our own most generous impulses or overwhelm us with too much giving. The most pleasant of arrangements is the kind of relationship in which each partner feels slightly and affectionately indebted to the other, so that each gives freely and openly. The sharing is a stand-in for the trust and mutuality of the relationship.

Perhaps we can remember an occasion on which someone extended an invitation to a restaurant, giving us the impression that we were to be the guest—and then announced our share of the check. Even more disconcerting, perhaps, is the occasion on which someone chooses the restaurant, orders expensive dishes on our behalf, and then expects us to pay. Many of us women, generally lighter eaters than men, will recall times that we ate very inexpensively, only to have the check split evenly among the party, giving us a sense of having been taken advantage of. Such situations are difficult to know how to handle diplomatically, and they can mar a new friendship irreparably.

Suppose now that you and a friend are having dinner in a restaurant that you can both comfortably afford. Your friend's spending and eating pattern will undoubtedly affect you, and vice versa. Whose invitation it is, what you order, how you enjoy it, and who pays are miniature dramas reflecting the mosaic of our inner relations to money and to the people with whom we are sharing it.

Think now about the last such dinner you shared with a friend.

- Did you scan the menu primarily or exclusively for the prices?

- Did you deny yourself a glass of wine or an appetizer you really wanted?

- Do you think your friend did?

- Conversely, did you spend lavishly, ignoring costs, and then peruse the bill ruefully, wishing you hadn't?

- Did, perhaps, your friend?

- Do you and this friend usually prefer to split the bill exactly, or do you tend to take turns paying?

Now think about other friends with whom you share such meals and outings. Is your pattern different with some friends than with others?

It can be revealing to consider what situations, and with whom, we most often pick up the bill. Perhaps it is because we have eaten with dear friends toward whom we feel generous and indebted. Perhaps we are trying to show off. Perhaps we are in an expansive mood. Or we may be buying love or social credit against next time.

- To whom do you give most often?

- What are you receiving in the giving?

- How deep or shallow are the gifts?

- Have you ever regretted giving a gift?

- Why?

Like the primordial tribal exchanges of goods and favors, money is ultimately a symbol of the possessions and power we command. The giving of money or gifts therefore has to do with our relationship to the receiver; reciprocity, exchange, temporary indebtedness in some form, lies at its heart. We are aware that generosity untainted by personal need is exceedingly rare. We bring wine to friends' dinner parties, a statement of thanks for their effort and a wish to correct the imbalance in their expenditure. Our birthday gifts are carefully calibrated to the quality of our relationship and our understanding of the receiver. Gifts to our children state not only our desire to please them, but our deep wish to be connected to them. Such gifts are not only for the benefit of the children, but for ourselves as well, as reassurance our ties to them when we want or need them will be there. We tend to remember and give to those who remember and give to us, and invest a little or a lot of care and forethought, depending on our relationship to the receiver.

MONEY AND FAMILY

Phyllis, forty-three, a successful small-town real estate broker, wanted to separate her joint bank account of twenty years from her husband's but could not imagine how to do it without appearing untrusting or hostile. She just felt a desire to control and keep track of what she earned and spent, in part because she was tired of having to explain every out-of-the-ordinary expenditure to her husband and in part because she felt that the old arrangement suited an outmoded self-image of the dependent wife.

Then her father died, leaving Phyllis a small legacy. Sharing with her husband her excitement at having money of her own, she opened a new account. He was indulgently amused, if a bit puzzled. This was a gentle introduction of greater independence into the marriage. Eventually, further steps were easier, like going away to a weekend workshop in real estate financing and taking a course in first aid at the local college. Although sometimes her husband was uncomfortable with the changes, Phyllis handled each situation carefully, and she was able to protect their long and stable relationship.

If you are part of a couple, think now about how you each respond to money. Are there important disagreements over spending priorities, level of spending, or money management? The deepest values about possessions and the money they represent may be shared wholly, partially, or not at all.

- Is one of you a big spender, the other a bargain hunter?
- Is one a divester, the other a hoarder?

These combinations can often work as balances and counterpoints, if they are recognized and welcomed as such. Marriages in which neither one has a clue about bank balances or in which both people are compulsive savers of paper bags and bits of string tend to be less resilient and adaptive to life's changing circumstances.

Now think about how finances between you and your mate are arranged. At one extreme, your partner may have allowed you to assume all responsibility, or at the other may have defended the exclusive right to know and decide. In fact, your growing competence and sophistication need not be a challenge to your partner but an added area for sharing.

- In your relationship, who makes which financial decisions?

- Is money a charged issue?

- Does it seem to matter who makes more?

- Does it matter whose money gets used for what?

- How much sharing of purchasing dreams or financial worries is there?

In a relationship, secretiveness about money often spells deep trouble. Gary and Beth, for example, are both professionals; he is an orthodontist, she a nurse. They have been working in Detroit all their adult lives, managing over the years to raise two children, buy a suburban house, maintain two cars. They share many values: the priority of the children's education, commitment to high standards in work, caring deeply about their respective parents, including, in recent years, helping to support them. But the financial arrangement is flawed. For complex reasons, Gary needs to keep his investment picture so private that it has long since become a taboo subject. In reaction, Beth has withdrawn confidences from him. Their stern contract continues: Gary pays for the ongoing family expenses, Beth for all educational and recreational expenses. Each takes care of his or her own car. Gary is alternately lavishly generous, taking the whole family out to an expensive restaurant, and miserly, unwilling to countenance a much needed new washing machine or a loan to a teenage child for a camping trip to California. Beth feels as though there must be an inner demon in Gary, who holds on to money and metaphorically counts it in the dark, making all members of the family wary. Their children will freely borrow small amounts of money from Beth but will never ask Gary for help, knowing that even if he were willing, there would be emotional strings attached. They have learned from experience that at first he won't give or lend, no matter what the reason for the request; then suddenly he offers, too late, and is hurt because they won't accept. This has distanced all of them from Gary. Beth now has her own pension and savings account and is beginning to work her way toward a separation.

Sometimes one partner may think little can be changed about ingrained, destructive patterns such as concealment, power plays, or total scatteredness. Then we need to try and figure out what this pattern symbolizes: it may be a metaphor for anxieties, some inner disorganization, the need to control, or unresolved trouble in the relationship itself. With understanding we can sometimes remake these patterns.

THE ACTUAL MONEY IN OUR LIVES

As we make changes, from remaking our nests to going back to school to traveling somewhere on an adventure, we must also make the financial decisions that are the building blocks for these changes.

Often, our histories leave us ill equipped to do so: it is the exceptional woman who was taught to be clear, forthright, and informal about money. Some of us may have been led to believe that money, or discussion of it, is vulgar—that we should not be curious or inquisitive about wills, salaries, benefits, and savings. If we were in traditional marriages, most or perhaps all finances were in our husbands' hands. "The bacon" came in the form of weekly or monthly household expense allowances. We did not manage big blocks of money; instead, we were experts at economizing by improvising and substituting. Those of us who worked outside the home, often as single mothers barely making ends meet, had to balance our sense of earning power against the clear cultural message that we ought not to be the primary providers.

As a result, we may now feel incompetent to deal confidently with practical money decisions. For example, we may fear that we may be cheated if we buy property or invest, unable to rid ourselves of the cultural stereotype that these financial activities are the province of men.

Identify your level of knowledge and confidence. Are you

a. Knowledgeable and relatively unconflicted in the area of money management?

b. Fairly knowledgeable but puzzled about sophisticated areas like stocks, taxes, or second mortgages?

c. Not very knowledgeable but confident about your ability to learn?

d. Not knowledgeable, helpless before tasks to which you feel unsuited?

e. Feeling that someone else is, or ought to be, taking care of you?

If you answered yes to c, d, or e, the problem may be simple inexperience, lack of information, or lack of interest. Now, perhaps suddenly, we are confronted with a new set of life circumstances. We are forced to grow up quickly and become responsible for this part of our lives. Or we may simply want to take charge of our own finances. We balance our own checkbooks; we pay attention to the mortgage; we learn to organize our receipts so that we know what to bring to the tax preparer; we find out what our insurance coverage—

automobile, health, property, and life—would actually pay for if we should need it. Clarity in planning and more concrete information are our goals.

For years, Kay's husband and his accountant took care of all financial matters. Every year she dutifully signed the tax forms without curiosity; she deposited her own earnings in their joint account. She rarely looked at bank statements and was only mildly disapproving of her husband's risky ventures into the stock market. Then divorce, division of assets, and the sale of the house made her urgently aware of her own ignorance about money.

The first tax year, her new accountant shepherded her through the filing process. It was agony, and Kay needed to return repeatedly with bits of information she had misunderstood or mislaid. She had not even known to bring W-2s and 1099s with her. Slowly she built a new vocabulary: she learned about assets, capital gains, mortgages, and interest. Over the next four years, as her knowledge increased and anxiety faded, Kay became reasonably confident at tax time. She still has no wish to prepare her own taxes, but this year instead of her long hours of muddled agony, it took her only three hours to organize her papers and add up her figures. The tax interview took forty-five minutes, and her supportive and amused accountant commented that she had good reason to be proud of herself.

Almost all financial advisers, estate planners, and accountants have the same first advice: Make an income and expenditure balance sheet for a typical year. This need not be more than approximate; as the chart emerges, a new sense of knowledgeability will replace hit-or-miss hope. We gain a new sense of control and the courage to make informed decisions about how to save or spend money to best suit our needs now.

a. If your balance sheets show that you have income beyond that needed for essentials:

- Do you usually spend your extra income on such pleasures as eating out, vacations, or shopping for delicacies?

- Do you let it sit in an ordinary bank account?

- Do you invest it in stocks, CDs, or retirement funds?

- In what proportion do you use these three options?

b. If your income and expenditures are just balancing, a crisis could topple you. A cushion is a necessity. What areas of expenditure could be reduced?

- Gifts and entertainment?

- Clothing?

- Vacations?

- Other things?

A look at your balance sheet will tell you.

c. If you spend more than you make:

- Do you rely on loans, credit cards, and delayed payments of bills?

- How can you change your expenditures, if at all?

A major new solution such as an extra job, renting out part of a living space, or investigating government subsidies can be options you have not yet explored. Frances turned her flair for sewing and mending into a small weekend business at home; Loretta converted her house and garden into a baby-sitting center for three children.

Alice rented her lakefront house for the summer and moved into a boarding house next door. It was wrenching to watch a strange family have picnics, boat, and sun in her space while her clothes and beloved knick-knacks were boxed away. But after the decision—it was this or sell the house—she became a firm, methodical landlady. She bought sublease forms from the stationery store and wrote her own riders about cleaning, maintenance, and damage. These were all new issues to her. As her life changed, Alice learned to manage her money and to become more sure of herself and her boundaries in the process.

Like Alice, our financial concerns change as we pass through the stages of life. Who, at twenty-five, is going to give more than a passing glance at a pension plan, Social Security, or retirement housing? Who, at forty, dares to be without health or auto insurance? Who, at fifty, has not considered pension plans or IRAs? Who, at sixty-five, is not well aware of her Social Security benefits and her future income?

For people of all ages, good financial planning involves providing for the disposal of our assets after death. If we have been meaning to make a will but haven't gotten around to it, we are among thousands of women who put it off. The prospect of our own death flutters in the wings, far away or close at hand. "Inevitable," says the mind. "Impossible," responds the imagination. "Frightening beyond speech," whispers the soul and heart. Yet one of our life tasks is to become increasingly at peace with the idea of the ending and to "die consenting," as the Greeks put it, with the legal issues resolved. The omission of a will can mean utter chaos.

Jeanne died a long slow death of multiple sclerosis at the age of forty-three, leaving two young fatherless teenagers and a country house. By long agreement, Joan was to be the executrix of the estate and the guardian of the children. For weeks after the funeral, she and the children searched for a will through six filing cabinets; there was none, although there were dozens of substantial savings accounts in as many banks. The sorting process took many months. Meanwhile, the children had to become wards of the state and live on survivor benefits. Two years later, when the estate was settled, Joan was formally appointed guardian and she and the children could begin more financially predictable lives. The house was sold and accounts were unfrozen to create money for the children's education. As the whole estate gradually became known, the children were able to live more than comfortably through their remaining high school and college years.

We have all heard stories like this, where lack of a will causes hardship, delay, and, worst of all, permanent injustice. Denise, divorced young, had lived for ten years with Frank. They had never felt it necessary to marry. He was killed in an auto accident, leaving no will. Because his first wife had not remarried, his estate passed to her, including the house and car. Denise was totally unacknowledged, and some of her own possessions were even preempted as part of the estate.

Many women neglect to speak with their families of their ideas about the future. How open have we been about our picture of our lives ten, twenty, or thirty years from now? Perhaps we have dreamed of moving to a southern climate or always assumed that we would sell the big house and move in with one of our children. Our thoughts are relevant to their lives. Of course, such matters may be difficult to discuss, not only because we would prefer not to think about them, but because they probably would, too. "Oh, Mother, you'll go on forever," they say, entering into friendly collusion with us in denial and permitting the lack of a plan to continue. However, our sense of clarity in organizing our futures, as well as our sharing with them of what we have in our insurance policies and our wills, can create a mature new platform for open communication with them. Ancient sibling rivalries, secrets, and favoritism tend to be resolved in the light of our openness and fairness.

Have you made a recent will? Wills get out of date surprisingly quickly; executors move far away, become estranged, or die; intimacies change, family members' needs change. Where once an estate would be equally divided among two growing children, now perhaps there are grandchildren and property to allocate among them. Never mind if you are only thirty and have few assets and no life insurance. You do have some possessions and perhaps some cash. Many people do not realize that the cash assets of single people who die intestate are automatically confiscated by the state! If your estate is not complex, then it involves no more than a brief visit to a lawyer, with relevant papers listing assets in hand.

If we have gaps in information about the financial situation we may encounter in our future lives, getting things in order to make a will can be an important threshold for reflection and reckoning. Our denial of the changes of the coming years alienates us from ourselves, as our unspoken worries sap the vitality we could direct toward making positive choices. Getting a sense of control over the actual inflow and outflow of money eases the vague anxieties and, of course, makes planning more realistic. It also can override and contain the destructive emotional baggage about money that we may carry with us.

Now, as we twist the two strands of money together again, the strand of our feelings about it and that of the actual flow of it in and out of our lives, the resulting rope may be stronger. We may have a new sense of conviction and satisfaction about our relationship to money. We have learned to recognize and name our idiosyncrasies, including the unwanted patterns and ways in which we keep ourselves ignorant, the ways in which we use money as a weapon or allow others to use it against us. We are more aware of the means of self-protection available but not yet availed of by us—and our threshold of action is now clear to cross.

□

MINITASKS

You may want to answer the first few questions posed here right in this book or in your journal, if you have chosen to keep one. As always you should explore the issues of your choice; remember not to overwhelm yourself by trying too many of these minitasks at once!

Money and Inner Life

1 • Which of the following describes your childhood impressions of money available:

a. consistent poverty

b. variable, but just making ends meet

c. comfortable but careful

d. comfortable

e. affluent

Now describe your adult understanding of the actual situation.

2 ▪ In one or two sentences, describe the dominant emotional attitude to money of the following:

Father:

Mother:

Spouse:

Children:

Other important people:

3 ▪ Have these people influenced your own relationship to money? Have you adopted any of their patterns or reacted to their patterns in a negative or compensatory way?

Yourself Now

4 ▪ How in harmony is your actual flow of money with your feelings about your control of money? Draw a line between the sentence on the left and the sentence on the right that describes your situation.

84

I have too little.	I feel powerless.
I have enough.	I have some control.
I have more than enough.	I feel powerful.

5 ▪ Underline the words that describe your usual reaction when your expenditures are greater than your income: panic, chronic anxiety, devil-may-care reliance on credit cards, resentment at restrictions on your standard of living, acceptance or even enjoyment of the challenge of living less, other:

If you wish, describe these reactions further in your journal.

6 ▪ Underline the words that describe your feeling when income is greater than expenditures: a sense of comfort and safety, guilt at a burden that you would like to be rid of, excitement at a ticket to adventure and luxury, guilt toward those who have less, dreams of quitting work, dreams of buying things, dreams of giving things away, other:

7 ▪ Test the limits of your attitudes toward money:

a. Browse in a thrift store if you never go, and make yourself buy something.

- What was it like?

- Would you do it again?

b. Browse in the fanciest store in town if you never go there, and buy something, even if it's small.

- What was that like?

- Would you do it again?

8 ▪ Rate yourself on the following scale as to intensity of concern with money:

    a. very money conscious

    b. somewhat money conscious

    c. average

    d. not too concerned

    e. unconcerned

    f. so unconcerned that you are careless

If you are at either extreme, is this a source of

- Inconvenience?

- Worry?

- Distress?

- Something else?

Describe this further in your journal.

Yourself and Others

9 · Think again about your family, friends, and closest associates. Rate some of them on the scale used in Minitask #8.

10 · Do you find it easiest to establish financial relationships with people whose pattern is closest to your own?

Or is it easiest with people whose patterns are different from yours?

Is your pattern very different with some people than it is with others? Recall, if you can, important incidents that established or changed these patterns.

11 · Try, as a onetime exercise, to adopt radically different behavior the next time you and someone important to you share an expense: paint the town red, your treat, if your penny-pinching friend brings out the Scrooge in you; stop yourself from reaching automatically for the check with your friend who always seems perfectly content to let you pay.

Practical

12 ▪ If you do not prepare a balance sheet of income and expenditures once a year, do it now. Divide a page of your journal. Make an approximate expenditure list for this year on one side. On the other, give a rough estimate of your income from all sources. How are you doing? Are you surprised by the results? Is your sense of anxiety or security justified?

13 ▪ Do you have a financial file? If not, buy an accordion-style file large enough to house other files. Make sections separating insurance, taxes, property papers, investments, and whatever else is important. Under insurance, include health, house, car, and life; under taxes, put your receipts and balance sheets, and so on. On a page in each file, write down the important contents, including pertinent telephone numbers and addresses.

14 ▪ Try reading one insurance policy each day, underlining the main points. Write down the terms or concepts you don't understand. For example, does your health insurance continue if you retire before sixty-five? After sixty-five? What are the terms of your policies? For illness, do they include hospitalization? Intensive care? Accident? Disability? Slowly, policy by policy, figure them out. If you can't unscramble the policies yourself, go to or telephone your bank, accountant, or insurance broker and ask for help. Remember that you are fully entitled, as a consumer of their services, to ask for explanations!

15 ▪ Now do the same for taxes. If you usually hire someone to do your taxes and you are "no good with numbers," sit quietly with last year's return, write down words and phrases that you don't understand, and get help or buy a primer. Tax handbooks exist in simple language. Don't try to do too much all at once, and don't get stuck too long on any one point. Feel free to browse. With time and repeated exposure, the concepts will fall into place.

The purpose is not necessarily to become a tax expert or to be able to do your own taxes, but rather to overcome any feelings of helplessness or confusion you have around tax time.

16 ▪ Are you clear about what your financial situation is likely to be in five, ten, fifteen, or twenty years? Have you been avoiding the knowledge because you are afraid you may not be able to manage? Or because you are confident or indifferent, based on no knowledge?

Locate all pertinent documents and data: pension plans, IRAs, other investments. If you are older and don't have any information about Social Security, go to the Social Security office for a copy of your payment record and ask for help in estimating your eventual benefits. If you are a possible future heir (of your parents, husband, lover, or whomever), what do you know about their provisions for you?

17 ▪ Have you written a will in the last five years? Write one now (no legalese necessary) in your journal. Are there information gaps? Ambivalences? Write them down. Write another version. Then call a lawyer or get a write-your-own-will form.

18 ▪ What would your life be like, in the best of all possible worlds, ten years from now?

- Where would you be?
- With whom, if anyone?

- How would you be spending your days?

- What would your financial situation be like?

19 • What about twenty years from now?

20 • What about thirty years from now?

21 • When you are seventy-five:

- Where would you like to live?

- With whom?

- What are your physical vulnerabilities likely to be?

- What are your financial vulnerabilities likely to be?

- How much caregiving will you probably need, and how do you visualize receiving it?

5 · Minds, Hands, and Senses

The mind is like a parachute; it only functions when open.

BUMPER STICKER

THE THRESHOLD YOU MAY WISH TO TRAVERSE OPENS OUT ONTO the paths of new ideas, skills, and awareness. At any age, and at any point in our lives and careers, the rewards of new learning are incalculable. They can range from the security and satisfaction of gaining a greater mastery of our homes and environments to the general sense of enrichment that comes when we explore the liberal arts and sciences. We focus now on expanding our knowledge, acquiring new practical abilities, and honing our perceptions.

The first steps to take include:

   a. identifying the kind of situation in which you can learn best;

   b. defining an area to which you are drawn, whether by past history or present curiosity or need;

   c. finding one small corner of that interest in which to begin.

IDENTIFYING LEARNING PREFERENCES

We each have a unique way of learning. Some of us are drawn to the written word, others to people. Some have good visual minds and think intuitively and spatially, others are analytically logical and linear. Some like to soak in information without preparation, learning by osmosis, while others like a structure for which they can prepare with formal facts.

These two preferences are sometimes called "instrumental" and "expressive" aspects of the self. They are present and, ideally, in balance in all aspects of life, including ourselves, families, and groups. Everyone is constantly balancing her instrumental and expressive sides, focusing in turn on structured, clear ends and supportive, nurturing means. For example, we strive to keep our lives organized while infusing them with love and laughter. We take time out from an urgent meeting or phone call to soothe a child or attend to a crisis; we use play as an opportunity to teach or learn.

Remember the grade school teacher for whom we would have written any number of poems or book reports? She was probably among the very rare individuals who used both knowledge, the instrumental side, and love, the expressive side, to inspire us. Most of us are not so evenly developed and have learned over time to emphasize one of the two modes.

- Do you tend to be happier when you emphasize analysis and results?

- Or do you tend to emphasize feeling and process?

Adrienne's preferences and strengths lie in the instrumental sphere. She likes organization and prefers written assignments for which she can read ahead and prepare notes. She finds it hard to speak extemporaneously in front of others. Now she is taking a music history class, and she loves the independent listening and memorizing for the weekly fact quizzes. Dorothy, on the other hand, tends toward expressiveness. She lives

in a close-knit suburban neighborhood and has an easy bright-
ness that attracts many friends. She loves volunteer work of all
kinds, feeling energized when she gives to others and runs
meetings. Yet when it comes to writing down a formal pro-
posal for a new day care center, she feels anxious and at sea.
In choosing a learning situation, Dorothy would be most in
harmony with herself in a small group where there is much
participation and involvement between students and teacher.
However, although it will seem less natural for her, she might
decide to develop her instrumental side by taking a large lecture course with a lot of anonymous written work.

Consider here your own learning preferences, whether you
want to master a field of knowledge or learn to use a computer
or a power saw.

- Would you rather watch and learn?

- Or would you prefer to figure something out from written instructions?

It does not matter what aspect of skill or knowledge you
choose, as long as you throw yourself wholeheartedly into a
situation in which you can learn: the act of learning will in
itself make you feel vibrant and growing.

FINDING AN AREA OF LEARNING

If you are unsure about what you might wish to learn, one
way to begin is to reconnect with old interests. We may want
to consider what we may have put aside or neglected out of
deference to those closest to us. One family member's expertise can often exclude participation by others. In a long-ago
childhood, a sister or brother may have carved out an area of
competence or claimed a field, and we may unconsciously
have chosen to pursue other things, reluctant to intrude on

occupied territory. Later, in marriage or partnership, a division of labor and interests often develops: you mow the lawn, I do the laundry; you choose the music, I keep up with literature. This often works out efficiently, but it can be limiting. We give up the opportunity to explore ideas, come to believe we are not capable of certain skills, and limit sensory experience. We are holding ourselves back out of respect, fear, avoidance of competition, or the need to cope with an overfilled life.

Elaine, married early to an older man, is now a young widow of forty-six. She gets great enjoyment from looking at family albums and wishes that sometimes it had been she making the choices behind the camera. She realizes now that her husband was a rather poor photographer; many of the pictures are not well focused or are badly composed. Yet during their long marriage he strongly asserted his position as master of the family technology. He would have felt threatened if Elaine had tried to share the camera—indeed, he once blew up when she picked up the camera and pointed it toward him to take his picture—and she felt that such conflicts were hardly worth it. Now she has enrolled in a photography course and is delightedly recording the first year of her granddaughter's life. Her daughter, also without camera experience, has begun taking pictures, too—and she and her mother are thinking of setting up a joint darkroom.

If we have children, another fruitful way of getting in touch with our hidden loves and ambitions is to consider how we are guiding their interests and career choices. Most of us encouraged our children to study subjects or fields that we secretly or unknowingly wished we could have pursued for ourselves. The ballet mother's attempt to live out her stage fantasies through a daughter who is desperately trying to please is an extreme example of a common phenomenon. Think now about your own children's choices. Perhaps they have responded to your wishes, explicit or implied. Or perhaps you yourself made choices that reflect your parents' interests. We all know mu-

sicians who were encouraged by parents who could not act on
their own passions for music or linguist/travelers who are living
out their parents' dreams of seeing the world.

Vicarious living is a risky business, and it cannot, even
under the best of circumstances, provide the satisfaction we
might feel if we were experiencing something for ourselves or
practicing a skill or art with results we feel are our own. Suppose, then, that you revive an ancient ambition. You may
object that you cannot now expect to become a scientist like
your physicist son or a concert musician like your violinist
daughter. Your own early childhood dreams of being a balle-
rina or actress may seem even more absurd and distant. But
you could connect yourself now to the theater, for example, by
volunteering to raise funds or take tickets for a struggling theater group. By defining your purpose realistically, in a spirit of
exploration and enjoyment, you should be able to approach
your old field of enthusiasm, become involved with it in some
capacity, and answer some of the questions that you have put
on hold.

MINDS

Born to left-wing professor parents who taught English at
one of the first black universities in the United States, Julia
grew up rebellious in the anti-intellectual 1960s. The turmoil
in the U.S. education system and a deep interest in theater
contributed to her decision not to go to college. She won a
series of summer stock apprenticeships. Then, at a crucial
juncture, her parents withdrew their financial and emotional
support of her dreams of an acting career because they thought
it would be too hard a life. At around the same time she met
and married Steven, a brilliant community organizer, and
they had a son.

To help support the family, Julia needed to work. Her lifelong ease in university settings made it natural for her to find
a job as an administrative assistant in a college history depart-

ment. Meanwhile, her dreams of a theater career died, as she was pulled in other directions by the demands of motherhood and then by the very sudden and tragic death of her young husband from a heart attack. Later, as a single mother with a college-age son, the university job became even more important, for it helped pay for his tuition at film school.

But at forty Julia was at a frozen point in her own life: she was desperately bored with her work, but the thought of attempting a return to the theater was acutely threatening and painful. At the same time, although she occasionally took courses, usually on data management for her work, she retained much of her old ambivalence about the value of a conventional university education. Still, she could not help being terribly embarrassed by her situation: new acquaintances assumed she must be a professor because of her sharp intelligence and her sophisticated way of presenting herself.

Julia's internal demons kept holding her back from making a choice between a committed return to theater and a committed return to school; as a result, she wasted her intelligence on the irritations of departmental infighting.

Then last summer she had an opportunity to become a research assistant to a professor who had a grant to write a book on street theater and revolution. Julia's background proved invaluable, and the professor insisted that she be given academic credit for an independent study with him on the subject. Suddenly Julia realized that she was on her way, not only toward the degree whose omission had always nagged at her, but also toward the field she had secretly wanted most to explore: theater history.

The world of education, both abstract and practical, is open to adult women as never before. We are going back to school by the hundreds of thousands. Community colleges and four-year colleges, now competing for students in a buyer's market, have noticed our outstanding track record for serious commitment and invaluable classroom contributions. We have a steady focus, an iron will to succeed, the discipline of our maturity, and the capacity to juggle many roles simultaneously.

Still, we have many kinds of resistance to learning new things, one of which comes from social stereotypes about what is appropriate for adult women. "I can't learn anymore," we protest. "I can't remember facts the way I could when I was younger." It is often true that adults learn new material more slowly than children, but this can be counteracted if we are selective about what we learn, write things down, use mnemonic devices, and avoid memorizing facts that can easily be looked up. There is much in our favor, as adult learners: we have a wider context of life experience into which to integrate new knowledge, so what we learn often sticks with us.

Phyllis has never worked outside her home. She has seven young grandchildren and loves being with them. Her enjoyment led her to dream about working as an aide in a nursery school. She enrolled in her community college, taking courses in developmental psychology, literature for the preschool child, and reading readiness. She discovered, somewhat to her surprise, that her parenting and grandparenting experience gives her memory hooks on which to hang almost everything she is learning. She finds very few concepts new to her, but the courses are giving her a vocabulary in which to organize them. Most of her classmates are in their late teens and early twenties. Much of the material is unfamiliar to them, and they must work to memorize and apply new concepts in a vacuum. In a study of the "terrible twos," Phyllis found herself the class expert, with psychological and physiological knowledge and helpful strategies for handling tantrums with age-appropriate games and toys.

Another common source of resistance to achieving new intellectual goals or skills comes from our sense of practicality. As we mature, we usually become increasingly concerned with the business of making our livings, maintaining our homes, and raising our families. We thus dismiss areas of knowledge that have little immediate bearing on our daily lives.

Minds, Hands, and Senses

At thirty-six Becky is a highly successful creative director of a New York advertising agency. It would never occur to any of her friends to wonder about her educational background: her achievements speak for themselves. Yet Becky is ashamed that she had only one year of art school, especially because her Ivy League–educated husband is very proud of his university and has many friends who like to reminisce about college. When these conversations occur, Becky retreats into silence, convinced that she is inadequate and cannot keep up.

Recently, when Becky began to think seriously about going back to school, her fears overwhelmed her. When someone persuaded her to enroll in a continuing education course in basic writing at Columbia University, she was convinced that she would be unable to handle even the pro forma entrance examination. She made the excuse that the demands of her job would make it impossible for her to attend class regularly and that she could not justify studying anything that was not connected to her career. In fact she was dying to go but absolutely terrified.

Not one of her friends doubted that she would be admitted easily, but her acceptance was an astonishment to her; even more surprising to Becky was the teacher's enthusiastic support and her outstanding final grade. Now she is the equivalent of a first-semester junior, slowly working her way, one course at a time, toward the B.A. that is so important to her sense of confidence and pride. Her boss is very supportive, letting her leave work an hour early twice a week, and he has promised Becky a promotion because her work, enriched by the art history classes she is taking, has been outstanding.

New credentials *do* have their practical side. They can help women never employed outside the home gain their first professional identities or help refurbish skills for a mother going back to work. There is a great need for librarians, dental technicians, statisticians, and secretaries, to name just a few professions. Going back to school can also allow us to make career shifts or upgrade jobs. An assistant in a nursery school can take early-childhood education courses and become the head teacher, a social worker can qualify for Civil Service status, a legal secretary or paralegal can become an attorney.

As with all new thresholds, it is best to start small and slow. Let the idea of taking a course or workshop simmer while you browse through the catalogue. Remember that reading a catalogue is not a commitment to take a course, it is merely exploring the idea. As you leaf through, note semester starting times, costs, and registration deadlines. If the idea of going to school fills you with anxiety, see if auditing is permitted. That is a far less formidable starting place.

As a child, Janice was bright in a brilliant family; today, one brother is a research scientist, another an economist. Janice studied French and became quite fluent during a semester abroad, dreaming about a career in French literature. But she married a young professor and had children early, putting aside her dreams. At academic parties she felt ill equipped to join discussions, secretly humiliated that she had no field of expertise.

Then, when the last of her children went away to school, she signed up for a course on recent trends in literary theory, taught by a brilliant visiting professor from the Sorbonne. Since the thought of writing papers terrified her, she elected to take the course on a pass-fail basis. But after the professor discovered her linguistic ability, he praised her in class and asked that she read the materials in the original French. She soon knew that she not only could cope with college but would love it. Three weeks into the course she decided to take it for a grade. She is now in college full-time, a French literature major with a minor in Italian. Her son, a history major, is a year ahead of her, and they exchange ideas and have even taken a course together.

As in Janice's case, learning a language can be a unique way of opening our minds to new sounds, ways of thinking, and cultural differences. Consider picking up one of the languages you studied or heard in your house as a child, a language you know but not fluently, or a language you have never studied but are curious about. Whether through formal college courses, adult education classes, or at home with records and tapes, the process is an exciting one even at the beginning level.

HANDS

Practical Skills

If going back to school is not for you, there are many other ways in which you can stimulate yourself to new learning. There is a vast world of practical skills to master.

Harriet and Dan married very young and set up house in a dilapidated cottage outside Kansas City. In the beginning, neither had much experience shopping and cooking or fixing doors, leaky roofs, and falling plaster. Gradually Dan, a computer systems analyst, learned to use tools and understand wiring and plumbing. Harriet developed many homemaking skills. She was soon expert at putting together calm, easy meals for everyone from drop-in friends to her husband's colleagues. The typical male-female division of labor had been established.

Then, when Harriet was thirty-four, Dan was killed in an automobile accident. Harriet's grief was accompanied by the shocking realization that she lacked even the most trivial repair skills. She did not know how to replace a fuse, unstop a toilet, change a washer, or fix a flat tire. Dan had also quietly taken care of all the financial decisions and responsibilities. Harriet's terrible sense of loss became linked to an urgent desire to overcome her helplessness and fill the huge gaps in her practical knowledge.

Harriet decided to learn Dan's skills. She approached the task systematically, enlisting her friends, children, plumber, electrician, mechanic, and accountant. It was hard work, but so absorbing that it allowed her to suspend her acute awareness of Dan's absence. Two years later Harriet continues to create lovely meals and an easy ambiance. But she also has a new air of confidence, as she casually mentions her new abilities. These include long-distance driving, keeping an accounting system, and using Dan's drill and saber saw.

For Harriet, circumstances and desire combined to push her toward mastering new skills. But we need not wait for tragedy. Many of us may be tired of searching for someone else to repair, carry, and fix, of having to telephone for appointments, wait for husbands, or impose on friends and neighbors. We may now feel a powerful urge to be able to rely on ourselves for tasks someone else—husband, son, mechanic, or handyman, it is almost always a man—has performed for us. It gives us a tremendous sense of victory when, for the first time, we paint a room, fix a toilet, or replace a torn screen. Gradually the toolbox becomes a friend. We learn the special qualities of a Phillips screwdriver, the different properties of Super Glue, epoxy, and Elmer's, how to mount a picture or a closet hook, and more.

Self-reliance in fixing things can begin with something as simple and financially rewarding as remembering that list of stain removers for blood, tea, wine, and grass. You find yourself less dependent on the dry cleaner, and your cleaning bills go down. You are delighted to have solved the problem on your own and begin to wonder what else you can fix by yourself or demystify.

Estelle is in her late seventies and she walks slowly, with the aid of a cane. Her grandchildren knew that she had trouble coming in from the garden to answer the telephone on time and worried that in her haste she might trip and fall. For Christmas they gave her an answering machine. They promised they would set it up for her, but when the last car pulled out of the driveway at the end of the holiday, she realized they had all forgotten.

For several weeks the answering machine sat in its box, unopened. When Estelle mentioned the gift to her friends, most of them said they'd never be able to figure it out. Then one day, having missed two calls in succession, Estelle put her glasses on, opened the box, and took out the instruction manual. The parts were diagramed and labeled, in large print. Step by step, as if coloring by number, she followed the directions, plugging the machine into the wall and the telephone into the machine. She discovered that there was a button for "Record," another for "Play," others for "Fast Forward" and "Rewind." She realized that the machine was basically just a fancy tape recorder. It was time to use it: with many false starts, she followed the exact wording of the suggested message and made her first, very self-conscious recording.

As weeks went by and she became increasingly comfortable with the machine, she was able to adapt it to her own needs. She programmed it to answer on the first ring: "Hello, this is Estelle. Please don't hang up, because I'm probably at home. I'll come to the telephone as soon as I can."

Estelle's victory over the answering machine prepared her for the next intimidating gift that came her way: a VCR. Hooking it up proved quite complicated, but Estelle had learned that patience and obedience to the manual would probably solve the problem. After many days of experimentation and frustration, she had figured out how to use most of the functions. She felt almost silly that she had always had such respect for men's know-how about sophisticated gadgets; in fact, as she told all her friends indignantly, "Those men were just following instructions!"

Carmela, another woman who won her battle with technology, lives in Berkeley with her second husband. There is a troubling recurrence of miscarriage and postpartem depression among the women in her family, dating from the time of her great-grandparents. Since then, an aunt, a niece, and a cousin have also suffered from this kind of depression. Carmela wanted to explore the family history by writing it down, both for her own sake and for that of her daughter. But the project was anxiety-laden because it evoked Carmela's own underlying depression. She never seemed to be able to get started. The pencils, pads, and little tables she had set aside for working on the memoir lay untouched day after day. She filled her days with activities so she would always have an excuse not to write. Guests piled in for lunch, tea, and supper; friends from the East Coast came for three days and, with her encouragement, stayed for weeks. The morning hours she had allocated to writing seemed to evaporate.

Her husband, at first sympathetic and then a bit impatient with Carmela's constant talk about something she hadn't even started, tried to help by buying a personal computer with a simple word-processing capability. At first this seemed only to give Carmela an even better excuse: she told herself and everyone else that she would begin to write as soon as she mastered the computer, a time-consuming task that she claimed she would take up as soon as her whirlwind of social obligations let up. Her well-intentioned husband learned word processing, but that backfired; suddenly the computer seemed to have become his area of expertise, and Carmela stayed even more firmly away, just as she stayed away from "his" stereo system. Perhaps, like the proverbial ballet mother, he had bought the computer because he really wanted one himself.

A wise friend steered Carmela toward a class at a local computer store. Sure enough, after just two sessions Carmela began to master and enjoy the new skill. She found she especially loved the polishing work, the sense of perfecting a page or a paragraph incrementally, tidying a little bit here, a little bit there, as the mood struck. But she needed something to polish. She hastily typed a few paragraphs about her family, focusing primarily on the computer and its capabilities rather than on what she was writing. There on the screen, first in very rough draft and then with increasing refinement as days passed, emerged a short, fictional piece about one of her ancestors.

Carmela works on her project for at least an hour every morning now, turning away guests during that sacred time. Friends have learned the schedule; they don't telephone. She now has a calmness that always used to elude her, and she claims, with vastly increased self-knowledge, that the new technology may have made her a happier person by far.

In another area of practical skill, cars and driving, we women must often work hard to overcome stereotypes of help-lessness. Some older women were lucky to learn to drive at all; younger women know how but still usually know little about how the engine works or how to make repairs. Brothers and boyfriends were at home in the tangled innards beneath hoods; we were not invited. Then when we had to go somewhere, there was usually some man who wanted to drive. The car was connected to his sense of masculinity; we yielded, perhaps gratefully, to him. We often gained a profound, socially in-stilled conviction that there should be a man at the wheel.

If driving is so threatening to you that you have never learned how, there may be no avoiding driving school. Despite all the excuses and delays, most nondrivers know in their hearts that learning to drive is probably indispensable. Some-times we need an "excuse" to take that first step. Take the case of Carolyn, a fashion magazine editor. She grew up in an academic household of modest means. A battered old car was always her father's sacrosanct area of power. There was never any question of her mother's learning to drive, even less of Carolyn's. As an adult living in New York, Carolyn never needed a car.

Then, two years ago, her brother died, leaving Carolyn a remote and beautiful cottage on the Virginia shore. She was faced with an awesome dilemma: learn to drive or give up the house. The house proved an incentive powerful enough to overcome years of resistance. Carolyn took three driving courses and finally had the courage to take the test. To her own amazement, she passed. Almost a year went by before she surmounted the next obstacle: she bought a battered used car just like the ones her father had loved so much.

To this day she remains a nervous, erratic driver. She would never dream of taking the car to the city. But during summers on the beach she makes brave five-mile forays to the post office, fish market, and other people's homes, experiencing each trip as an adventure and each homecoming as a small victory.

Crafts

Handwork is an area of practical skills that many women find greatly satisfying, both as a sensual experience and as a mode of self-expression. Perhaps you have always wished you could weave, knit, or do needlepoint but never seemed to have enough time. Displaying what you make, or giving it away, can be the source of a very special sort of satisfaction. There are other benefits as well: if you tend toward restlessness or have time on your hands, hooking a rug can quiet the soul and keep you in one spot for a while. If you have an impulse to revive a hand skill, or to try one for the first time, a local crafts store is one place to start. The people there can probably refer you to the teacher or situation you are looking for.

As a young mother Eunice was a distractible and delightful companion. She raised similarly active, high-energy daughters. The family shared an interest in making things; kitchen tables were often covered with homemade paste and scraps of construction paper. Birthday and holiday gifts were almost always handmade. When the children went off to school, Eunice volunteered in a nursery school, surrounding herself once again with paints, clay, and fabric.

She had to give up the work with children when she was fifty-five; a lower-back problem made stooping and lifting impossible. Now, at seventy-one, she has severe diabetes and is confined to a wheelchair. But her sense of color and her pleasure in using her hands have never left her, and she has found a perfect medium for her artistry. Working slowly, from a tray laid across her chair, she creates vivid, surrealistic collages. Friends bring her wool, beads, and interesting objects to work with. Her old interest in making things has enabled her to learn to sit still and has made her disability more bearable; and her pieces are exhibited and sold in local crafts stores, bringing her a little extra spending money.

Perhaps you wish you knew more about jewelry making, a satisfying craft that has attracted many women. The tools are inexpensive, space requirements are small, and you can practice the craft in your own time without leaving home.

Patricia does this. Thirty-eight and divorced, she has moved to a scenic crafts village in Mexico with her father, who is dying slowly of Alzheimer's disease. There she can easily afford luxuries for her father like daily massages and nursing care; they sit together and enjoy the warmth of the sun.

At first Patricia had time on her hands, so she cast about for a focus. Fascinated by the Aztec dress and decoration she saw in Mexican museums, she began to research the aesthetics of different tribes. Starting small, she made herself one necklace, then another. Soon she began to run out of space for her shells, beads, and bells, and she turned a side shed into a workshop. Now there are not enough hours in her day, as she fashions necklaces, medallions, and earrings, fusing the archaic and the modern to create unique jewelry. She sells from her home, but only to those people she feels can understand the deeper meaning of her work and its connection to Aztec art.

It seems strange, but despite her father's situation she has never been happier. His imminent death has taught her to savor the life they have together, and she pours her sense of reverence into her art, feeling fulfilled in its making.

SENSES

The extension of our senses is another threshold that we can cross onto a new path. We may consider ourselves unobservant or nonvisual, relatively indifferent to scenery, art, architecture, color, and light. We may think we don't have an ear for music, that our palate is not refined, or that we are not sensual. We may open up a world of new pleasures and sensitivities by setting ourselves the task of noticing, listening, tasting, and touching with more attention. Some of us may in fact not see or hear as well as we wish. Rather than passively accepting the weakness or inattentiveness of our perceptions, we can discipline, educate, and explore them.

Sight

We think we observe our worlds, but in fact we take in only a fraction of what is around us. Training ourselves in deeper observation can give us endless pleasure.

Perhaps you have a friend who is more visually inclined than you. Mary and Angela have been friends for four decades. Angela was taking a course in calligraphy, an art form about which Mary, a college librarian, knew nothing. One day, as Angela practiced, Mary watched. Mary admired the special pens for special strokes, the attention to rhythm and flow. This totally new visual experience inspired Mary to search her attic for a copy of the medieval *Book of the Hours*, a family heirloom. Holding it gently and turning the colored pages, she became aware in an entirely new way of printing and the decorativeness of written language. Eventually her interest led her to ask for a transfer into the rare books collection, where she can use her new visual awareness every day; her warm connection to medieval books continues to expand and delight her.

Going to new places or doing different kinds of activities can also be literally eye-opening. Pat, for example, a mathematician notorious among her friends for being in an absentminded world of her own, went off one August on a birdwatching trip in Maine. She came back glowing and enthusiastic, with a newfound capacity to notice and identify birds. She had also learned to love hiking, to be comfortable outdoors in the rain, and to live in close quarters with others, for the first time since college. Now she leads her binocular-laden friends on expeditions into the woods, sharing her excitement at birdcalls, markings, flight rhythms, formations, and nest styles and materials; one of her friends has become as passionate about birdwatching as she. Their awareness of detail has become far more finely honed, as they observe and listen more exactly; they are paying attention not only to birds, but to small movements and sounds in general.

Listening

Reconsidering our habits of hearing can lead us to enjoy fields that we have neglected or left undeveloped: music in its many forms, oral history, storytelling, playgoing, or poetry recitation. Perhaps you will want to approach this sphere by buying or upgrading a sound system. Dusting off your old musical instrument could be another first step; there are many amateur chamber music groups that meet in people's homes. Books on Tape can be a fresh new way of enjoying literature, as well as of enjoying the ancient tradition of oral literature.

As a child, Maria lived in a house filled with classical music. A flutist father and cellist mother were always practicing and listening, refining their own performance styles and criticizing those that had no integrity. But if poor classical performances were bitingly dismissed, pop and jazz were outlawed heresies. Maria was not permitted to play top-ten radio or to watch *American Bandstand* or *Soul Train*.

Then in college Maria began to date Jeff, a part-time jazz critic. Slowly, with his help, she began to appreciate a new range of musical experience. Jeff helped her recognize the ground rules and beauty of the different styles. She learned to love the great players and to applaud great improvisation.

Maria, already a good listener, branched sideways; Gertrude learned to substitute listening for sight. As Gertrude reached her late eighties, reading, a lifelong joy, became increasingly difficult. As she was bedridden with arthritis, the long empty days passed slowly for her; even television was only a blur as her sight dimmed. Then her daughter learned that the Library of Congress lends oversize tape decks, with easy knob controls and extra-loud volume, to the sight- and hearing-impaired.

After the machine arrived, Gertrude listened willingly but showed little interest in learning how to use it herself; she would even call other family members to turn the tapes over for her. Then one day, when she was alone in the house, the tapes arrived for Jane Austen's *Sense and Sensibility*, one of her favorite books. She was so excited that she figured out how to insert the tape and turn on the machine; she went on to the second tape without help. It was a deeply moving experience for her family to come home and find her lying in bed with her earphones on, her eyes closed, and her expression utterly rapt.

We too can work on expanding our intellectual, manual, and sensory horizons, learning to experience a fragrance more deeply, noticing a beautifully carved chair, concentrating on the craft involved in how Flaubert describes his characters, becoming completely absorbed in Mozart or jazz. At this threshold we open ourselves to see, hear, think, and use our hands with greater awareness. As we make the first steps down the path to hanging bookshelves for the first time, listening to an entire opera, or writing the first paper for a new course, all our usual fears and resistances will present themselves. Jump right over; you can begin to explore with one or two minitasks that seem attractive and manageable to you right now.

☐

MINITASKS

You may want to start here with the first exercise, as it will help you to define which areas you will want to pursue. Once you have discovered what your preferred pattern of learning is, you can go on and choose one or two minitasks (or more) that complement your tastes.

1 ▪ To clarify your preferred patterns of learning or working, circle the letter preceding the descriptions that best describe you in the following statements.

I usually learn best

a. from a lecture or written instructions.

b. in a one-on-one situation or a small class, where I can watch, interact, and imitate.

In general, I learn best when

a. I am given a clear task that I can finish by myself.

b. I create and complete a task with the help of others.

I work better when

a. I have clear lines of authority in which I report to one person.

b. I share responsibility for my work and report to my co-workers.

I would prefer to

a. lead a meeting, determine the agenda, and implement the decisions.

b. be part of a meeting in which others participate as fully as I do.

If you selected mostly a. answers, you primarily favor an instrumental style. If you selected more b. answers, you are primarily expressive. These preferences can guide your choices of learning situations.

2 ▪ If you love the idea of going back to school but cannot imagine yourself actually doing so, try visualizing and writing down your worst fears about what might happen. Then put your writing aside and march down to your local community college, language institute, business school, or work-shop center. Locating the place and walking around inside the building will bring the possibility of signing up a major step closer. Next go to the registrar and ask for a catalogue. That is enough of an achievement for one day. Let the idea simmer.

3 ▪ If you live far from any college or institute, you may have to structure your own education. Here is an example of how to start: Choose a personality or event of special interest to you, such as Eleanor Roosevelt, the Grand Canyon, or herbs and spices. Read a book on that subject, then move on to others. Suppose you have always been interested in Queen Victoria and have only a vague impression of a passionate marriage, many children, and a very long life. Find a good biography. This may lead you to other books about the period. Expand your area to include information about the clothing, furniture, and architecture of the time. Perhaps eventually you will make a trip to England or join the Victorian Society. Your exploration of the life of an extraordinary woman may well infuse your own life with new vitality. Draw up a plan for yourself to focus on one writer, historical period, or issue that has intrigued you for a long time.

4 ▪ Divide a page of your journal into three columns. In the first, write down practical skills you have, including tool uses and repairs. In the second, write down the skills of which you are less confident and the skill problems you solve with hit-or-miss uncertainty and anxiety. In the third, write the skills you would like to have and repairs you would like to be able to make.

Choose one from the middle column to practice and one from the last column to try for the first time. Make it a priority during the next week to find a simple how-to book, with diagrams, or a friend or a neighbor who can teach you. Be sure to make it clear that you want to learn, not just watch.

5 ▪ Make a list of the machines and appliances you own: food processor, cassette recorder, TV, VCR, and the like. Divide them into three columns: those whose functions you understand completely, those you understand only partially because you haven't explored them or have some hesitation or fear, and those you understand not at all and have perhaps never used. This week, play with one from the middle column and one from the last column. See if you can expand your understanding of their capabilities.

6 ▪ In your garden or a local park, take a short walk. Choose a tree, shrub, plant, or stone and, for five to ten minutes, study it minutely, noticing its structure, color, shape, smell, feel, and how the light falls on its. Close your eyes and memorize its qualities. Go again to the same object on another day, at a different hour. Notice new qualities, the effect of different light. Call up the image of this now deeply familiar object when you need a peaceful inner moment.

7 ▪ Lie in bed and, with closed eyes, listen. Concentrate on the varieties of sounds, sorting and isolating a few from the general buzz. Do this each day for a few moments. Work on increasing the range of sounds you can distinguish.

8 ▪ As a concentration exercise, select a favorite record or tape. When you are alone in the house, settle down comfortably, unplug the telephone, and listen. As soon as your mind wanders, turn off the music. Come back to the same record or tape on another day and see if you can focus on it longer. Be honest. If you have drifted off, turn it off and try another time with the same tape.

6 · Travel

The real voyage of discovery consists not in
seeking new landscapes, but in having new eyes.

MARCEL PROUST

VICKY, A THIRTY-FIVE-YEAR-OLD SCULPTOR ORIGINALLY FROM
Santa Barbara, had lived in New York City since her graduation from art school. Sociable, talented, and ambitious, she
had been vaguely unhappy ever since her divorce two years
earlier. The competitive hustle of the New York art world left
her constantly on edge, and she found the fragmented urban
singles scene extremely unpleasant. Living alone now in the
too expensive apartment she had once shared with her husband, she felt desperate for a change.

She agreed to spend a month in Mexico visiting her father,
who had just retired there. Although widely traveled, Vicky
had never been particularly interested in Mexico, and she soon
began to have regrets, dreading the dislocation and the prospect of sharing space with her father for the first time since she
had left home. Until the day of her departure, she continued
to paint to any friend who would listen drastic pictures of the
horrors probably awaiting her.

It turned out that she was completely wrong. Her father had rented a home in a scenic, cobblestoned silversmithing town. The two-bedroom apartment opened onto a private courtyard with flowers, cacti, and a parrot. As the slow-paced, sunny days passed quietly, father and daughter began to rediscover each other as they talked about the past, about her dead mother, and about the solitariness of both their lives. Vicky saw with fresh clarity that her situation in New York had become intolerable.

Then one evening, in one of the friendly local cafes, she met Ed, an outgoing, witty American who was studying Spanish in Mexico for his import-export business. After leisurely evening strolls in the square, weekend expeditions to a hot springs and a leather-manufacturing town, and a sultry passion consummated on a moonlit beach, they both seemed to feel that their romance was very special.

Vicky and Ed began exchanging intercoastal visits. He urged her to come live with him in San Diego. This coincided with the impending expiration of her lease. With a sense of taking an enormous personal and professional risk, she decided to go. She knew that whether or not the romance continued, the trip to Mexico, the developing friendship with her father, and then the blossoming relationship with Ed had been much needed catalysts for change.

Vicky's Mexican journey led to a major shift in her life course almost by chance. Yet going away can be one of the most powerful tools for transformation that we have available to us. Physical and emotional distance can help us muster the resolve for actions we have been contemplating for a long while. At the same time, breaking away from habitual patterns to experiment with new ones may in itself be a welcome challenge.

A journey can be divided into three phases, each with its own pleasure and anguish, challenge and routine:

1.   Deciding where, when, with whom, and for how long to travel; preparing to leave our nest and taking the steps to make the voyage a reality.

2. Making the trip itself, with its unexpected discoveries and the self-scrutiny that dislocation invites.

3. Returning home, with its own reverse cycle of reentry, when we are seemingly the same person but intangibly different.

These three events blend together in actual experience and, later, in memory. But each has a distinct quality, a separate challenge with its unique anxieties and pleasures. Think now about your next trip, whether you are actually planning one or simply imagining what the next one could be:

- Why are you going, beyond relaxation and a change of scene?

- Does the excitement lie in not knowing what you may experience?

- Whom you may meet?

- What you will learn?

- Or do you prefer to predict rather definitely what your personal harvest will be?

In fact, every phase, from the difficult planning stage through the return home with fresh perspectives, is ripe with opportunities to know ourselves better and gather energy for change in other aspects of our lives. For most of us, a decision to travel is also a decision to postpone painting the house, trading in the car, or moving to another apartment. But this can be well worth it: the journey is an intangible investment in the self.

ATTITUDES TOWARD TRAVEL

Our ideas about traveling to foreign countries, other states, or even the next town are formed during childhood. For those of us whose parents took us with them on trips, going away to unfamiliar places may have worry-free connotations of pleasure and adventure. Or we may have been left behind when parents traveled, so that we fantasized painfully about strange places off limits to us. Even now departures and arrivals may evoke emotional responses rooted in our early sense of abandonment. Perhaps one parent went places more than the other, and we developed two different internal models, one of safety and one of adventure.

Shelly's mother feared traveling. She made preparations even for short trips days in advance, with frantic anxiety about packing, tickets, weather, and schedules. Always late, she would run for trains while Shelly and her brother struggled to keep up, afraid of losing sight of her. This had a lifelong effect on Shelly, who to this day displays a similar pattern of elaborate preparation and lateness. Although she understands the connection between her mother's behavior and her own, she cannot travel alone and learned long ago that trains, planes, and schedules catapult her into an immobilizing panic. To her credit, she does travel but almost always brings companions who can assume responsibility for the arrangements and ease the experience for her.

By contrast, there is Lila. Her parents ran a vast wheat farm and rarely left Illinois, but she had relatives who were missionaries and visited frequently, returning from assignments in Africa and the Middle East. One aunt had a sabbatical every seven years, and she sometimes took Lila, her favorite, with her on her long vacation travels, once to Alaska and once to Micronesia.

Out of the five children in her family, only Lila developed into a secure traveler; her siblings live to this day near their family farm, deeply attached to the soil. Lila, however, became one of the first American airline stewardesses, and she married a sailor-cartographer. Her second baby was nearly born on the boat from which she and her husband were exploring the coast of Tierra del Fuego. Now a seventy-two-year-old widow, Lila continues her globe trotting, reading travel books and visiting far-flung exotic places, bringing carry-on luggage only.

Depending on our family histories and other experiences, then, our degree of adventurousness will be different. Our task now is to find the right fit between ourselves and our prospective journey, challenging ourselves just a bit more than we are accustomed.

TOURISTS AND TRAVELERS

As you read the following stories of four different women's travel needs and aspirations, consider which solution is closest to the one you chose for your own most recent trip:

Sarah, a deeply religious single woman with little travel experience, is deacon of her local Minneapolis church. She signed up for a tour that was open only to members of her congregation, to visit the mission churches of Southern California. All the planning was done for her, and since Sarah had grown up in Los Angeles she felt secure about the destination as well as about the other travelers. Even so, the preparations for leaving home were wrenching for her. She fretted about leaving her cat in someone else's care; faced with the prospect of missing several community service gatherings, she agonized over who could take on her responsibilities. Never had her daily routine seemed so dear. She even considered canceling the trip. But in the end she was glad she had not given in to her anxieties; the mission churches were a deep and lasting inspiration to her, and she returned even more enthusiastic about her work at home. Now she is helping to plan next year's trip.

Joanna signed up to go on a twelve-day rafting trip on the Colorado River with the geology department of the university where she works. She knew the other participants slightly before the trip started, since they had all taken a course in river geology the preceding spring. None of them had been rafting before, however, and they all had unspoken anxieties about physical safety and endurance. Joanna, a rather shy woman who had never been married, had her own special fears on top of these: she was particularly nervous about being in close quarters with near strangers for so long.

On the first night by the river's edge, Joanna pitched a tent far from the others; this was for privacy rather than shelter, as it rarely rained. But she soon overcame her fear; on the water, she learned to rely on others and give help as needed. This lesson about interdependence was as precious to her as the memories of the vast canyons and their spectacular rapids. By the end of the trip she was sleeping near the others by the river's edge for coolness, beauty, and conviviality and had long since given up the unnecessary tent.

Rochelle is a business administrator at a small college. She uses her vacation for a different adventure every year. A veteran of a Greek ancient history tour and a Swiss learn-to-ski vacation, she joined a group bike trip on Cape Cod. Not only had she no idea who her companions would be, but she had not ridden a bicycle for long distances since she was a child, and she worried about whether she would be able to keep up. Giving herself a month to prepare, she rode her new bicycle greater and greater distances every day, ignoring the sometimes painful soreness in her leg and shoulder muscles. Through a minicourse at a bike shop, she learned how to oil her chain, grease her gears, patch leaks, and change tires.

To her great delight, her training paid off. She not only kept up, but was able to help others with emergency repairs. As the group bicycled from town to town, they focused on the architecture of old houses, a new area of observation and knowledge for her. Friendships developed quickly, and Rochelle remains close to two fellow cyclists to this day. When weather permits, the three of them go on their own weekend outings.

Helen is unusually independent, able from childhood to fill many contented hours alone outdoors. A free-lance registered nurse in her late forties, she decided to go backpacking in Nepal, a country that had attracted her ever since an interest in Eastern religions led her to a book on Himalayan temples. She took care of every arrangement on her own: visas, shots, plane and bus tickets. She perused traditional guidebooks primarily to learn which overbeaten paths she should avoid and to obtain information on climate; she studied Nepalese through tapes and prepared herself physically by trekking at high altitudes near her Denver home.

A Western woman backpacking alone is an anomaly in many parts of the world, including Nepal. But the mountain peasants quickly recognized Helen's self-assurance and responded warmly to her. She accepted many offers of hospitality in cliffside hamlets, using her nursing skills and cache of supplies to give small gifts of medical treatment.

Sarah, Joanna, Rochelle, and Helen span the range of voyagers, as exemplified by two definable extremes, "tourists" and "travelers."

As pure tourists, we bring our cultural, social, and personal styles with us. We observe foreignness through an invisible, protective glass bubble. We stay in American-style hotels that allow us to regulate how much exoticism we wish to absorb; we choose tours and cruises whose members help us carry our culture along; we transport our familiar nests by buying or renting a camper. We are attracted by group expeditions, with their offers of convenience and security. We feel more comfortable when we surrender responsibility.

Planned itineraries are good options if we have little or no experience with travel: anxiety about language and loneliness is cushioned by the tour guide, who deciphers our new environment for us. We endow this person with authority and quite a lot of actual and emotional power. As pure tourists we become, for a time, worry tree, fed and cared for—a challenge in itself for those who rarely allow others to look after them.

At the other extreme, as travelers we are on a quest for self-discovery. The model here is the solitary wanderer who learns the language, stays in a room with a local family, and enters as nearly as possible into local life. She examines and challenges the familiar through daily confrontation with stark or subtle differences. She temporarily adopts alien food, time rhythms, and even clothing, and explores the value systems and customs of that region.

For the traveler, financial limitations can be a spur toward more daring travels. The lack of money may lead us away from the heavily visited, expensive cities and resorts. There must be a willingness to arrive without a reservation and to find some cheap hotel or pension, to wait for the unscheduled second-class bus, to have an open-air market lunch of cheese and bread. These adventures can lead to chance encounters with strangers, fueled by mutual curiosity and friendliness. However, such travel does not come without its costs; at times there will be a sharp yearning for the familiar, as weariness with alien things weighs upon us.

Sonia, recently widowed and trying to get perspective on her grief, made herself go on a trip to Mexico. She signed up to go with a group of forty young seniors over sixty, to study Spanish for several hours in the morning and visit Mayan ruins and museums in the afternoons. Although from childhood Sonia had had a vague fear of Spanish-speaking people, she had never known any Mexicans except for an occasional cabdriver and, once, an affable and helpful plumber who came to her house in an emergency.

The first day in Mexico she found herself tense and watchful, suspicious of waiters, pedestrians, and shopkeepers. The experienced group leader presciently held a discussion about cultural prejudice. As the weeks flew by, the local people listened to Sonia's rudimentary Spanish, which they met with patience and warmth. Sonia's feelings were gradually transformed. Her appreciation of the gentle, philosophic, and cheerful qualities of the Mexicans she met had begun.

But one day she wandered into an unfamiliar place in the city and found herself in a panic. Whatever Spanish she had learned evaporated, and she stood uncertainly at a corner, looking at the alien street names. She felt as if she would give anything in the world to be back at home where she belonged.

A tiny Mexican woman selling fruit and pottery was watching her. She approached and gently touched Sonia's arm and smiled. Sonia found tears streaming down her face that she could not control and gestured helplessly. The woman took her hand and stroked it comfortingly. *"¿No habla español? Venga, venga."* She led her into a nearby restaurant and called someone to come out of the kitchen. After a few minutes of negotiation in broken English and Spanish, the man from the kitchen and the old woman walked two blocks with Sonia and pointed her in the direction of the familiar church on the square. Sonia found herself moved to kiss the old woman on the cheek, and they waved to each other with some regret. She found her earlier attitudes astonishing, when she remembered them.

Whether to be a tourist or a traveler is a choice. If we are looking for a pause in order to gain new energy for our lives, then perhaps we will prefer to emphasize our tourist selves. If we look to travel as a tool for insight into our lives and possible inspiration for changing them, we are exploring the traveler in us. But whether we go as tourists or travelers, we are at a threshold: we may now become more conscious of the process of making the decision to go, the preparations, the experiences we have while we are away, and our reintegration on our return. We may examine our usual patterns and experiment with making changes in them, even if this means we must deal with greater anxiety about variables that are unknown.

TRAVEL COMPANIONS

For each of us, there is a long process between our journeys in fantasy and the decisions that lead to actual departure. Perhaps the most crucial decision we must make about the journey is with whom we want to travel.

If we are in a stable relationship, traveling as a pair is likely to be a long-established pattern. Comfortable and predictable, the double cocoon offers a sphere of safety. We support each other, share experiences, comfort each other when plans go wrong. There are limitations, though. We reach out to strangers less often, because we are already self-contained; we experience the new environment less directly, because it is mediated in part through the perceptions of our companion. Furthermore, a dyad always involves compromise: Mary wants to explore new hotels and cities; Howard wants to return to that wonderful place they went last time. Eunice wants to look into local jewelry techniques; Henry wishes they were hiking in the hills above the city.

Many great marriage partners can be highly unsuccessful travel companions, and minor but regular separations can be crucial so that different needs can be met. Before the trip, couples may wish to explore this question so as to avoid conflict later on. For long-term partners, there may come a time to expand the repertoire of separate trips. We may welcome the challenge of planning adventures for ourselves, of learning to deal with time alone and independence from home. Experiences apart can refresh and honor a stale relationship or, sadly, point to the increasing gulf between us. The separate journey can even be a rehearsal for ending a relationship.

Travel with infants or young children can be manageable and even enjoyable. Most commonly, parents try not to introduce too many changes in schedule and menu, choosing to travel in a van or camper to replicate home life. Some people even bring along a helper to mind the children. But the most arduous family travels are possible: Jane Goodall and her husband raised their child among the great apes of Lake Tanganyika; others have raised children while banding birds in Antarctica. Fred and Jenny, a young couple passionate about sailing, took their five-year-old twins on a two-year round-the-world sail, making navigation techniques, fishing, and port visits a temporary substitute for more conventional schooling.

Traveling with adult children can also be a daring experience that can bring unexpected rewards. Far from the context of ancient family politics, we learn freshly about one another as we explore stimulating new places. Shared contributions of funds can become a symbolic equalizing, a way of canceling early power plays as we become friends able to reveal our limitations and strengths. A rediscovery of some of the activities that we enjoyed together years ago can remind us of the depth of our family bonds.

Sometimes, on impulse, we ask a friend or acquaintance to go with us, less out of a genuine wish to travel in that person's company than as a hedge against anxiety and loneliness. Before we extend the invitation, we might consider if our patterns are compatible or in conflict. How would you and your companion answer the following questions?

- How flexible are you about time and inconvenience?

- How much predictability do you like?

- Do you like to hook up with strangers or not?

- What are your attitudes toward smoking and alcohol?

- When do you want to go to bed and get up?

- How much do you expect to spend?

- What level of comfort and cleanliness do you expect in hotels and restaurants?

- What do you hope to get out of your travels?

Travel

The most unlikely combinations of people can mutually enhance the travel experience by balancing and stimulating one another. But travel dyads can also become prisons, if we discover that we are less well suited to each other on the road than we expected. Differences in inner rhythms seem to come out most clearly as people travel, creating major conflicts over such seemingly minor questions as how much time to spend in a museum or how early to start the day.

Imagine you have just arrived in Marrakesh after a grueling week of poor living conditions and bad food. Your companion seems to have come to Morocco only to shop. Back in Casablanca, tensions between you flared over whether she should buy yet one more rug to add to your already incapacitating luggage train. After one look at the filthy hotel, your companion announces that she can't take it anymore and is going home immediately. That is just fine with you. But at the American Express office, she discovers that she is unable to extricate herself from prepaid joint accommodations and restricted flights; you will be spending another two weeks together.

Such scenarios are not uncommon. Many of us choose companions based on factors that have little to do with the stress and exhilaration of traveling together.

Tina and Amanda had been friends for forty-five years. They shared baby-sitting and household projects like wallpapering, gardening, and making jam. One summer, when their husbands planned a fishing and hunting trip in Canada, Tina and Amanda decided that they too would go off on an adventure and selected a three-week package trip to London. They had thought they knew each other like sisters, but travel revealed otherwise.

The journey soon began to fall apart. Tina was afraid to go out of the hotel alone, would travel only by taxi, and liked to spend the mornings before an outing reading about the monument or performance they were to see. Not so Amanda. A restless soul by six A.M., she wanted to wander the streets and watch the sun rise over London Bridge. In a short time the two women had withdrawn from each other, feeling disappointed and betrayed, aghast at their mistaken assumptions about each other. They doggedly lasted out the whole three weeks, increasingly unable to converse about anything at all. To this day they have an embarrassed, strained relationship in which they pretend to a closeness that has been irrevocably lost.

An experimental weekend trip could therefore be a wise prerequisite to going off on a longer expedition, whether with a friend or as part of a new romance or trial honeymoon. You may find out unexpected things about each other, wide gaps in the values you hold or the expectations you have about the purpose of your travels. Or you may find that the short time spent together bodes well for further sharing of your lives.

Jean, recently divorced, fell in love with Ralph, a well-known painter fifteen years her senior. They shared many interests: gardening, scuba diving, and meditation. Living two hundred miles apart and busy with their professions, they spent the first several months of their romance indulging in short but passionate and fulfilling weekends at each other's homes. Jean secretly believed that they might marry.

Then they carved out three weeks together for a sailing trip in the Caribbean. Within less than a week, Jean's fantasies were dashed. Alone with Jean on the boat, with few activities to distract him, Ralph talked almost without break. Jean grew more and more introspective and silent. She found she had to sit facing him, make determined eye contact, and say, "Now it's my turn to talk," in order to stop the flow. Although Ralph regretted it, he did not seem able to control his lifelong habit of dominating the conversation. Deeply disappointed in their poor interaction, they ended their vacation early, still close friends but lovers no more.

TRAVEL ALONE

When most of us think of making a solo journey, we have many fears. We think of the possible loneliness, getting lost, or even encountering danger. But there are many rewards: aesthetic experiences can be deeper because our concentration is uninterrupted by the presence of others; casual conversations with strangers are more likely to take place; new acquaintances are more likely to become friends since there is no familiar relationship to depend on. Alone, the traveler is open to serendipitous encounters that can influence her journey for an hour or a day and her memories for a lifetime.

After a crisis there may come a time of fearing to be alone and then a time of withdrawal from people. Traveling alone can serve as a hiatus in which there are no social demands; it can also be a time to delay a decision about the next stage of life, a time for introspection and healing.

Kathy had returned to graduate school in clinical psychology at thirty-two. After three grueling years in which she worked as a night technician in a research laboratory and carried a heavy academic load during the day, she failed her oral examinations and was told she would be unable to continue her doctoral program. Devastated, she decided to go away for a while to avoid everyone's questions and sympathy. She wanted to think things over before applying to other universities.

She chose Utah, a place that she had found calming ever since her first childhood visit there with her parents. As she hiked alone in the dry heat, feeling sometimes lonely, sometimes exhilarated, and sometimes serene, she came to a decision to abandon her Ph.D. work for the time being. She realized that in trying to meet the financial and academic demands, she had given up friends, leisure, the possibility of a lover, and much more. The supremely beautiful rock formations and desert sunsets helped her see clearly that she wanted to move at a more peaceful pace. She began to forgive herself for her failure.

If we are thinking of going off on an adventure like Kathy's, we may have to make a conscious effort to overcome our own prejudices against women traveling alone. A hundred years have elapsed since social mores dictated that women not go out unescorted, but such deeply entrenched rules die hard. Perhaps we feel we are being watched, our lack of a companion judged or misunderstood. We hide behind a magazine while waiting for food, over- or undertip in embarrassment. We have an uneasy fear that our aloneness will be seen as suspect: people will think we have not been chosen, that we are unloved—or that we are looking to pick up a man or are possibly even a prostitute. As long as it is difficult to handle ordinary public situations alone while we are still in our home environments, it will remain daunting to contemplate a major journey.

The disapproval of women traveling alone can be very real, of course, and even dangerous. Our sensitivity to foreign expectations of dress, manner, and customs when we travel in certain places must be especially acute. However, the rarity of being a woman alone can sometimes work in our favor, stimulating sincere interest and helpfulness. We are unthreatening, and strangers sometimes identify us with their sisters, mothers, or grandmothers.

One strategy in uncertain social environments is to start with a group and leave it or start by visiting a friend. Ann, an experienced solitary traveler, has a fine solution to easing the difficult first few days. She visits foreign countries where she has friends or acquaintances, and she becomes a short-term guest. She never overstays her welcome, usually finding her own hotel room or apartment by the third or fourth day even if her friends are very hospitable. Her hosts always seem to enjoy her appreciation of sights and excursions that they have come to take for granted.

PREPARATION

For even the most experienced of us, there is likely to be a pretrip preface of general anxiety. Some of us focus these fears on an isolated concern, sometimes valid, sometimes not. Doris buys tickets months in advance, not only to save money, but also to quiet anxiety and firm up her commitment to go.

Travel

Frances puts her suitcase in a corner months ahead of a trip, periodically tossing things into it lest she forget them.

Elaine, a pediatrician, fell in love with another American during a conference in Europe. It was the first time she had cared deeply about anyone in many years. After their return to their separate homes five hundred miles apart, Peter visited her. Now she was going to his place, to meet his brothers and see his house. She was full of anxiety, but not, seemingly, about him or the visit: all of her fears centered upon the amount of time it would take to drive to the airport. This one short, uncertain leg of the journey had become a metaphor for the risk of a possible serious involvement with Peter.

Our preparations are also farewells, a series of closures. The decisions that commit us to a given departure date, mode of transport, and itinerary are often made with some sense of taking a plunge. We contemplate the approaching interruption of our daily lives, suddenly acutely aware that we will no longer have our morning coffee or tea in this kitchen, open our daily mail, go out for milk. We notify associates of our impending absence, prepay bills, put the car in a safe place, eat our way through the refrigerator. We clean out drawers and closets, complete desk work, balance the checkbook; we put things in order in such a way that we seem to tidy up our entire lives. As if living out our final days, we often make provisions for animals and plants, revise our wills or make them for the first time, take out insurance, put safe deposit boxes in order, entrust keys to family members, sublet or find house sitters. Although we know consciously that we will be separated from our homes only temporarily, we can't help feeling and acting as if it is possible that we may never come back.

We must also take leave of people. We separate from the mother who depends on us, from classmates, from the best friend whom we have been supporting emotionally during her divorce, from the new boyfriend who may or may not be waiting for us when we return. These farewells can be like early rehearsals for final good-byes, and they often seem to affect us far more than a short separation of a few weeks or months seems to warrant.

Now our hour of departure arrives. Our nest is spotless, our daily presence already erased. Then comes that strange moment of stillness when the leaving is over but the journey not yet begun. During the taxi ride or lift from a family member or friend, we are consumed by last-minute concerns. Did I remember everything? Call everyone? Shut off the stove? Leave my keys with the neighbor? We rifle through our purses one more time to make sure we have tickets, passport, and travelers checks. Perhaps we'll have the urge to call home from the station or airport to see if anyone is missing us yet or to say one last good-bye.

THE TRIP

Until we arrive, we may not know how we will react to the strange environment. Perhaps we will discover that we have overestimated or underestimated ourselves. On a group excursion there will often be one or two people who have made a mistake in the fit between themselves and the structure of the program. Perhaps they are uncomfortable in the new setting, emotionally or physically, and if they can't go home, they would rather stay as close to the hotel and their rooms as possible. Others feel unexpectedly at ease and chafe at the tight tour timetable that provides too many restrictions.

Lynne, a college professor on sabbatical, started out on tour of China's archaeological sites. Unhappy with seeing too much too quickly, she left the tour despite the huge financial loss, rented a bicycle, and went her own way. She had only a rudimentary knowledge of Chinese, but the local people proved endlessly curious and helpful; bicycles were so common a form of transportation that even a Western woman alone on one drew relatively little attention. Her decisiveness afforded her three months of wandering and a departure into independence that would affect many aspects of her life deeply.

On the other hand, among those traveling without structure, even the most experienced solitary traveler may find herself racked with loneliness, suddenly yearning for more consistent companionship, for an itinerary and a fixed goal on which to hang the day.

Fortunately, a characteristic of travel is a social openness that can lead to easy camaraderie and rapid, if usually fleeting, friendships. There is an eager exchange of information and backgrounds; intense, shared experiences of a few hours or days. Journeys are often shaped by the people we meet by chance. Couples for a time become foursomes; solitary travelers become pairs. We meet someone at the ruins who is more of an archaeologist than we: she tells us about the Mayans, we take her snorkeling for the first time. Another new friend takes us old-fashioned types to a local bar and we end up dancing until four A.M.; we give thanks by leaving him our sombrero to wear into the desert the next day.

Flexibility in itinerary can be essential if we wish to avail ourselves fully of the opportunities we may find. But most trips have a fixed end point, often dictated by the tyranny of round-trip restrictions or job and family responsibilities. The trajectory of weeks or months thus has an artificial end against which we count down the days, eagerly or regretfully as the case may be. It is worth reminding ourselves that it is only a ticket! Depending on whether duties at home and financial constraints permit, we may be able to go home earlier or stay longer.

- Have we bought a dated or open return ticket?

- Have we locked ourselves too tightly into a schedule?

- Will we long to go home sooner but doggedly, pridefully stick it out?

- Will we be on a personal threshold that needs further exploration?

Diana, an academic librarian, went to Florence during her summer vacation for a one-month course in intensive Italian. Classes, housing, and meals were prearranged through a program. It was a very secure plan for a first-time European adventure.

After the first two weeks, Diana found that the classroom study all day and meals with the same family every night left her little opportunity to try out her elementary Italian on the street, hike to hill villages, take the rickety local busses, and eat in the tiny, intriguing restaurants. She cabled home that she would be returning a month late and changed her ticket, paying the extra fifty dollars without regret. She continued to work intensively on language at the school but moved to a pension where there were no other Americans. She ventured careful phrases with her landlady, merchants, and waiters, daily making that ever less frightening leap from language on the page to language in the mouth. Her new acquaintances were flattered to be called on as teachers and seemed to share her sense of victory whenever she made herself understood.

After the month of school was up, Diana filled each day by exchanging language lessons with new friends and acquaintances and going with them or alone to see churches and frescoes. Halfway through the second month, however, her thoughts turned more and more insistently toward home. She recognized that for her the adventure was nearly over, so she changed her ticket again and did not force herself to stay the final six days.

Many trips thus have an inner timetable out of step with the external one. The courage to try ourselves out in new ways, learn from strangers, and encounter experience openly and deeply will take a certain amount of time that cannot be charted in advance.

As a way of reflecting on the people important to us at home, we may consider our habits of communicating with them. We can learn much about ourselves and our relationships if we ask whether we are calling or writing out of a sense of duty, homesickness, guilt, concern, a desire to reestablish or reconfirm bonds, or a mixture of several of these things. The periodic phone call, sometimes at great inconvenience, is a way of checking in emotionally. The postcard pile, with the "wish you were here"s and photographs that we hope will convey some of our visual experience, is a quick way of reassuring ourselves and those to whom we write that everything is all right and that the bonds between us still exist. Long letters can be ways not only of sharing what we are doing, but also of synthesizing what is happening in our inner lives, as we try to integrate the new people we are with, the places we see, the strangers we talk to or want to talk to and can't, and their differences with us and our worlds.

Still another link to our homes is the camera, that ubiquitous black box, for most of us a crucial travel companion. Check off on the following list what your camera usually means to you. Is it:

a. A way of bringing your experience back to those at home?

b. An aesthetic tool?

c. A way of opening conversation with local people?

d. A plaything?

e. A way of recording what you see so that you will be able to remember it better?

f. All of these things?

Most of us are well aware that photos and experiences are far apart, one being only a distillation of the other. But what we forget is that sometimes guarding cameras and lenses from theft, purchasing film, and having it developed can become annoying preoccupations. Sometimes everything we look at is judged as if it were a potential photograph. Furthermore, our ability to take pictures can give us the illusion that experience can be possessed or owned, as if it were a series of objects. In this sense, the camera can interfere with experience rather than contribute to it.

If you are a photography overenthusiast, try as a challenge to leave your camera behind for one hour or one day and see how dependent you may be on it as a way of mediating experience. On the other hand, if you never used a camera, or used it only rarely, try borrowing one for a day and shoot one roll. Carrying a camera may make you more sensitive to the essence of a place or a face.

We can learn much, too, about our feelings toward home by examining our gift buying more closely. Notice how individualized your choices are:

- Do you buy the same gift for many people?

- Is every gift intended for a specific person, or do you sometimes buy all-purpose gifts so that you won't discover you've forgotten someone?

- How much pleasure, guilt, homesickness, or other feelings are involved when you buy gifts?

- What does each gift show about your relationship to the receiver?

- Do you spend more than you can afford?

- Do you resent or enjoy the shopping?

As with the camera, it might be an interesting experiment for you to change your usual pattern. If you usually come home laden with gifts, try not buying any (before you leave, you may want to inform those who expect gifts about your experiment!); if you rarely bring gifts home, make a list before you leave of those you love and like and try buying gifts that you think will be meaningful symbols of what is between you.

THE RETURN

As we turn homeward, images of what we have left behind are woven into images of what we are heading toward, as we try to make sense of the new self in the old setting. We may need time to integrate our new experiences into our former lives so that we can resume with new energy and insight. We also may need to be particularly gentle with those waiting for us. They will undoubtedly be delighted by our return, but perhaps they have also felt unconsciously rejected by our absence. The moment of return is when the people we live and work with can most easily recognize us as someone who has changed, and it is an opportunity to establish new patterns with them.

The bags are empty, mementos unpacked. Giving the presents is a way of showing how we missed someone or perhaps apologizing for having left. It is a way of assuaging the discomfort of others as we reenter their lives; it is also a way of easing our own process of reentry with peace offerings.

The sharpness of the memories fades fast, and old patterns and routines begin. Getting back into our routine must include paying homage to our journey, our experiences, and our growth. The telling of tales and the time we spend alone reflecting on our experience are both important aspects of this process. We also listen, catching up on what we have missed, as the before and after are linked, with the help of the important others in our lives. We may for some time feel alienated from them, incapable of fully conveying what has happened to us and disappointed in some subtle way by the gaps in our understanding.

It can sometimes seem as if into the weeks or months away we packed a lifetime. We have gained a new sensitivity to our own culture and environment, as we created it, left it behind, and have now returned to it. We try to sustain the resolutions we made about changing ourselves; we try to hold on for as long as possible to the clarity we may already feel slipping away. We may have a sense of loss, as the images blur and the kaleidoscope settles into a few sharp pictures.

It may take days, weeks, or months to feel once again at one with our lives at home. The stronger the bonds we formed with the people we met, the more deeply involved we became in our adventure, and the farther away we went from home, the more time we may need to make the transition. Enjoy this time, for it is transitory and the insights are precious. We have been given this one additional threshold, the return, to learn and grow from.

□

MINITASKS

Is the preparation, the actual journey, or the return most difficult for you? You may want to concentrate on one of these three as you choose which minitasks to try out.

Preparations

1 • Consider your last three vacation trips, and using three different-colored felt-tip pens, circle the answers that describe how you went. See if there is a pattern:

Your Role	Degree of Structure	Companions
visitor (to a friend)	inflexible	none
tourist	some set, some unplanned	one person
traveler	unplanned	group

2 • Fill out this graph in relation to your most recent trip, and consider what your answers have taught you:

	Errors/Successes	Anxieties Overcome	Learned
Preparation			
Journey			
Return			

3 ▪ Imagine what your *ideal* next trip would be if you had unlimited time and money:

Where?

How long?

Degree of structure?

With whom (if anyone)?

What would you like to learn about your destination?

What would you like to learn about yourself?

Which travel anxieties would you like to overcome?

4 ▪ Imagine your next *feasible* trip.

What three places do you most want to go?

How long can you stay?

In which country or town will your budget give you the most possibilities?

Whom, if anyone, do you want to go with?

Can you find a solution that satisfies some of the qualities of the ideal trip you outlined in the previous minitask?

5 • If you are shy about the idea of traveling alone, try, just once, treating yourself to a nice meal in an exotic restaurant, preferably one whose menu is very foreign to you. Be aware of any fears you may have concerning your ability to ask questions about dishes that pique your curiosity and of any negative fantasies you have about others observing you.

6 • If you are eager to try traveling by yourself for the first time, go away overnight as a rehearsal for a perhaps much longer trip to a much more distant destination.

The Journey

7 • As you travel, spend fifteen minutes each evening, with or without a journal, reviewing the day and thinking about the pleasures and disappointments of it. Imagine how you would have spent the same day at home, with its pleasures and disappointments. Remember a different aspect of home life each evening: work, housework, pets, hobbies, each important relationship.

8 • Each day you are away, try to do one small thing you have never done before. Take an unfamiliar walk or bus ride, shop in the market using a few newly learned foreign words, try a new food, go snorkeling or folk dancing for the first time, sit in the square alone, *speak to someone new!*

9 ▪ Notice what parts of your life story you choose to tell strangers. What do you select, exaggerate, or leave out? Become aware of these self-presentations and try to emphasize a different aspect of yourself next time you need or want to give a capsule summary.

10 ▪ If you have a camera with you, try taking the kinds of pictures you don't usually take, such as nature shots, faces, night pictures, or abstractions. Notice how the camera affects your perceptions and relationships.

- What will the pictures mean to you?

- Will you look at them often at home, or will they sit in a box?

- To whom do you most want to show them?

If you discover that you are wasting undue energy and anxiety on photography, try leaving your camera in the hotel safe for a day.

11 ▪ Is the opportunity to shop determining your decisions about how to spend your time, where to go, and what to see?

If you are a shopping-traveler, make a resolution to buy nothing for a whole day and see how this feels. If you rarely shop for yourself, make a point of treating yourself to a small gift next time you are tempted to buy something for someone else.

12 ▪ Take some time alone outside the hotel every day, even if you are on a tightly scheduled tour or with companions. Notice your feelings of pleasure or vulnerability.

- Does being alone seem particularly difficult?

- If so, what or whom are you missing?

The Return

13 • The day before you go home, or on the journey back, make a short list of the ways in which you plan to change your patterns at work, at home, and in relationships. Start each item with "No more . . ." or "More . . ."

Keep this list near you during the first weeks after your return. Make observations, in writing if you wish, about the powerful cultural values and messages that flood in on you as you reaccustom yourself to your surroundings. For a time, be an observer and critic of your own culture. Try to hold on to the insights and resolutions you made while away. Notice roles and habits of interaction that you have outgrown.

14 • Soon after coming home, evaluate the details of the trip. What could you change about

1. Planning?
2. Companionship?
3. Luggage?
4. Money?

- Were you satisfactorily well-informed beforehand?

- Did you choose the right person or group to go with?

- Did you pack well?

- Did you manage your money well?

In your journal, pinpoint avoidable and unavoidable mistakes, for next time.

15 • Write down your new thoughts about yourself as tourist and traveler. Does your self-description have relevance for the other parts of your life?

7 · Loneliness and Solitude

I want to be alone.

GRETA GARBO

FOR YEARS SARAH WAS A BUSY SUPERWOMAN, JUGGLING JOB AND home. In the mornings she dressed impeccably for work, fed everyone breakfast, packed children's lunches, called the plumber, remembered to put daughter Carol's swimsuit in her school bag, took dinner out to defrost, fed the cat, found her husband's lost car keys, and called her hospitalized friend—all before eight A.M.

Now everything is different. Separated from her husband after an often difficult marriage, her children grown, she has taken a job as a student adviser in a new town in which she has no friends. Her days are stimulating, full of conversations with energetic and confused young people, but the evenings and weekends drift by in unnatural voids of silence. She lives alone, slowly healing from the breakup of her marriage. Faraway children, now involved in their own families and professions, visit her out of concern; Sarah limits her telephone calls to them, not wishing to remind them of her neediness.

She knows that in time she will develop colleagues, acquaintances, and friends and perhaps even find a lover. But for now her inner conversation with loneliness and solitude has begun.

Sarah stands at a rich threshold with a broad path before her that she needs to explore. She is confronted with a person she scarcely knows, a woman full of energy and skills, dealing for the first time with the unfamiliar, threatening phenomenon of loneliness.

Our aloneness is an opportunity to make peace, not with who we thought we ought to be, but with who we are. Time by ourselves gives us inner space in which to sift, judge, and integrate the past, synthesizing the lifetime of development, striving, and searching that has brought us to the current threshold of change. We can also use time alone to ready ourselves for some kinds of radical change, ritualizing the period in which we are still looking for answers. We may wish to pause on our thresholds of change, deliberately prolonging the moment before we commit ourselves to a path. An aid to our stillness is our choice to be alone.

Thinking about the distinction between loneliness and solitude can clarify the way in which we most commonly view being alone at this time in our lives. Loneliness is that feeling of wishing hopelessly for the presence of another or others, while solitude is the feeling of inner satisfaction while alone. We escape from loneliness; we long for solitude. Identical activities we do when alone can have an undercurrent either of anxiety and flight or of active enjoyment: they can be destructive or pleasurable, depending upon whether we do them in a spirit of loneliness or of solitude.

We begin the unfamiliar process of making friends with ourselves when we are alone. Our goal now is to strive toward comfortable solitude balanced by social interaction free from desperation and neediness. There are three complementary tasks here: the first is to deepen our capacity to be pleasurably alone; the second is to become increasingly selective and aware about how and with whom we spend the time with others; the third is to recognize our need for solitude and carve it out for ourselves in the midst of a busy day of work and interactions with children, husbands, and friends.

Do you have enough solitude in your life? Have you been clear to important others what your needs are?

When we are certain that we have a right to private time and space, however small, the means to creatively carve it out of a wildly busy life will emerge. Our certainty is more than half the battle.

If we are in transition from family to being alone, however temporarily, or if we are between jobs, these challenges have a painful and exciting immediacy. Conflicting cultural attitudes are at war within us. We have been led to believe that the ultimate stage of human development is autonomy, independence, and self-containment; but we also know that human beings, especially women, are profoundly social creatures whose survival and emotional wellsprings are rooted in the network of family, friends, and community. The American tradition emphasizes self-sufficiency as the value that is more desirable, mature, creative, and, perhaps, masculine. We admire the lone cowboy, the poet wrestling in isolation with self-expression, the brilliant professor or scientist lost in his own universe, the self-reliant adventurer.

We also admire Mother Theresa for her selfless service, the woman who adopts unadoptables, the battered women's counselors, and social workers reaching out to child prostitutes.

In fact, independence is inseparable from interdependence. The two principles enrich and inform each other. If we are alone, and we welcome and deepen our social commitments, our solitude becomes richer; conversely, if we are part of a couple or family, developing our capacities to enjoy solitude will bring renewed vigor to our relationships.

Paula, a high school science teacher, has a pattern of socializing that goes from one extreme to the other, but it works well for her. Long divorced, she lives alone, with her four grown unmarried children nearby. She is still their nurturant center. They drop in with their friends, stay over, celebrate birthdays, and drop off their laundry. Paula enjoys the motherly image and is proud of her ability to produce a quick meal for ten. On the other hand, she is utterly relieved when the house is finally empty; towels and placemats go in the wash, and the house subsides. She is "peopled out" and recovers slowly. Partly because she knows that there will be a next time, her solitude is richly enjoyed.

Many people keep themselves so busy that there are virtually no moments alone. Emma, for example, a sixty-five-year-old registered nurse and the administrator of a small nursing home, dreams of retiring, buying land, and building herself a small house. A childless widow, she has enough assets from her husband's insurance and her long working life that she could do this without financial strain. But she cannot bring herself to retire even though she is well aware of feeling physically exhausted, overwhelmed, and ready for a change. She fears that without the structure of going to work every day she will feel old and stagnant; she is terrified that she will be alone.

Pleasure in our own company is a learned art for most women. The social hum of girlhood, adolescence, courtship, motherhood, and work provide very few islands of solitude. It is still considered feminine to be dependent; responsibility for our safety is a task socially assigned to the men in our lives. There are few impulses or opportunities to walk, explore, go to a movie, or eat alone. We may define ourselves by our roles vis-à-vis others and by what others say about us as we perform them.

But then, at various moments in our lives and in various forms, we are all Sarah. Suddenly, after being too busy, we are not busy enough. "If only I could fit it in" is no longer in our litany; rather, our primary difficulty lies with our use of open time. The appointment books shows blank space, and we may become uneasy. Faced with unstructured hours or days, we don't quite know what to do, idling them away in activities that give us little sense of joy or accomplishment.

SOLITUDE AND FAMILY HISTORY

Some babies seem to arrive in the world with a well-developed capacity for self-contentment, while others become most alive only in the company of others. Perhaps, for whatever reasons, you were among those fortunate few who saw solitude as a welcome opportunity to amuse yourself. Perhaps you continue to use it as a gift now.

Rachel is one of the rare people who is almost equally content alone as she is with others. The youngest of three girls, she was excluded from the games of her older sisters except when she was made the victim. Left to her own devices, she spent many happy hours at the neighbors' farm, riding the mare and helping out; the rest of the time she played in her room with her collection of plastic horses, brushing them, saddling them, and creating pastures and barns. Animals were the truest and most reliable of friends.

As an adolescent, Rachel rode well in horse shows; during summers she was a riding counselor at a nearby camp. Now an adult, she has an active and successful life as a racehorse trainer. She continues to be quite satisfied to spend almost all of her time among horses, and although she is confident in human company, she is not in need of it beyond the companionship of a few close friends.

But for most of us, solitude is a difficult area that cries out for new skills and exploration. Zena, for example, hates being alone; she feels truly alive only when she is the center of attention. As a beautiful and talented toddler, she learned to sing and dance for the delight and approval of others. Her mother encouraged and spoiled her, putting her on stage for every visitor. But whenever she stayed with less indulgent relatives or had a free play period in elementary school, no amount of "go play by yourself for a while" could stimulate her ability to be contentedly alone.

Zena is now a well-known character actress who works fantastically hard to reach perfection in whatever role she is performing. However, she still has great difficulty being alone, hating the time in between plays in which she has lots of free time. She cannot read or watch a sunset alone; without an audience, she is lost.

- What were your childhood experiences with solitude and loneliness?

- Were you an only child?

- Were you one of many siblings?

- Was time and space to be alone a privilege?

- Was it a punishment?

- Was it the norm?

- Were you most content as a loner?

- Were you happier among many friends?

The childhood patterns may stay with you in adulthood as you choose paths that support and enlarge the original preferences. A quiet, self-absorbed, and observant baby becomes a butterfly collector, then a biologist. The extroverted babbler becomes a high school drama star, then a television producer. But experiences different from your family constellation may reveal new traits. Many a child quiet and lonely through lack of confidence has learned to enjoy the banter of social life, and many a talkative socializer has learned to think before she speaks and enjoy solitude.

YOURSELF, ALONE

Habits built as adults in using unstructured time depend not only on the preferences we bring from childhood, but also on our life situations. The young mother of four, in her rare moments alone, has a multitude of household tasks to accomplish. By contrast, after a grueling day in the office, the single lawyer can order takeout food and enjoy a long hot bath to unwind.

Look now at how you typically choose to use unstructured time alone at home.

- Do you like to putter and organize?
- Do you repair and build things?
- Do you prefer desk work?
- Are you happiest when your hands are busy?
- Do you sink into a book?
- Do you doze or daydream?
- Do you watch television?
- Do you get on the phone?
- Can you allow yourself leisure without guilt?

There are perhaps three common ways of spending solitary time. The first is in simple, ends-in-themselves activities like walking, resting, or listening to music. These allow you to daydream, remember, and plan. Joan plays games of solitaire every morning while she plans her day and jots down things to do; Liza has a two-mile evening walk with her German shepherds and gets ideas as they all bounce along. Mary likes to take long baths after work, scrubbing herself with a loofah while she thinks about her cherished garden, about what needs weeding and what to pick for dinner.

What are your favorite ends-in-themselves activities?

Then there are useful tasks. We all have areas of competence in performing routine jobs that have clear results and give us a sense of accomplishment. We fix and arrange our nests, dust and wash, clean out our desks and purses, straighten the bottoms of closets, make spaghetti sauce. Some of us like to spend time grooming ourselves, putting on makeup, setting our hair, or doing our fingernails.

What are some of your favorite useful tasks?

The third time spender is in self-development or self-refinement: study, exercise, reading, the practice of an art or a hobby. A needlepoint or reupholstery project, or the reading of a fine novel, has a useful purpose and an absorbing and pleasurable effect as well.

Do you have such favorite activities?

Of the three ways of spending unstructured time, which do you use most?

a. Ends-in-themselves activities?

b. Routine, useful tasks?

c. Self-development and refinement?

Has the balance among the three remained the same throughout your life?

Some of us are quite happy if alone and busy but are thrown into a panic if we are alone and idle. We become edgy and restless if our minds and/or hands are not occupied. One possible reason may be that we are trying to keep uncomfortable thoughts at bay: dissatisfaction with a job or a marriage, worries about an overstretched budget, anxiety about an unhappy, ailing father, angry impulses, or painful memories. If this description fits you, your threshold involves recognizing and naming the uncomfortable thoughts. This may be a long and difficult task that can often be helped by therapy. The first step is to acknowledge that there might be something inside you worth exploring so that you can someday become a person more at ease with herself alone.

We each have a characteristic way of dealing with that

feeling of empty loneliness that sometimes comes to all of us, no matter how confident and happy we usually are—the irrational fear that nobody loves us and that we are worthless. In another mood, open time would be a blissful gift, but when we are depressed it can be a nightmare. At such times we become engrossed in uninteresting television programs for hours or make automatic forays to the refrigerator for food we don't really want. Or even more self-destructive, we gorge ourselves or get drunk. We spend hours on the phone long after there is anything to say; we may even create or contribute to interpersonal crises, just for the satisfying sense of involvement with life. We fill our time with something, anything, just so there will be as little emptiness as possible.

DEALING WITH LONELINESS

People react to their loneliness in a variety of ways, from reaching frantically and desperately toward others to retreating into themselves, growing increasingly unable to reach out at all. When you are lonely, what is your usual response?

To begin coping with loneliness, think first about the situations and times you are likely to feel it most acutely.

- Around the time of your period?

- On weekends when you have no social plans?

- At a party or social gathering at which you are apt to feel isolated?

- When other people with whom you live exclude you for some reason?

- When our partner or lover is enmeshed in other things and has little time or energy for you?

- After a major argument?

- At some other time?

What are two self-destructive ways in which you have dealt with this recently?

If you know in advance that these times are coming and you may be vulnerable, there are strategies to adopt to help you move toward more successful solitude, depending on your usual pattern of coping. If, rather than be alone, you over-anxiously seek the company of others, even those who make you unhappy, your strategy is to find more projects and activities that you can do alone that make you content; if you are reclusive, your strategy is to find new ways of reaching out.

PROJECTS ALONE

Perhaps there are solitary activities that you used to enjoy or new areas that you would like to explore. Such activities enrich our lives and help us when we are alone not by choice but by necessity. Here are some examples of projects you can plan to do alone. Make sure to buy and organize in advance the things you may need. If you wait until the moment of despondency arrives, you may not have the will or energy to assemble what you need to distract and heal yourself.

a. Hang a shelf, clean a bathtub, paint a table, lay a new linoleum floor, or cook a dinner for future use.

b. When the despondency arrives, walk around your living space and decide on one area you want to make more functional or beautiful. Nurture yourself by fixing your nest in some fashion. Small acts may change your mood: washing blankets, mending clothes, transplanting a houseplant that has overgrown its pot.

c. Write a letter to someone dear to share what you are struggling with. Then go out and mail the letter.

d. Write in your journal, exploring your feelings now. Go back and look at other entries, as a reminder of other states of mind and of the progress you are making.

As you experiment with such projects and others of your own devising, you will develop new habits for spending time alone. Gradually, open time will come to represent opportunity, not emptiness.

SHOPPING

At those moments when we feel uncared about and alone, some of us try to comfort ourselves with a gift: we splurge on a scarf, a sweater, ice cream, or some other longed for but not essential item. We shop endlessly, often unnecessarily; a small errand turns into a major expedition. Some people believe that shopping is the best medicine for depression. But this powerful weapon may be either an effective way of cheering yourself up or a self-destructive source of temporary thrills. If for you shopping is sometimes a way of avoiding loneliness rather than of enjoying solitude, then it may be time to take a second look.

As an exercise in self-knowledge, think now about one shopping experience you had during the past week:

- Why did you go?

- Were the shopping stops planned or spontaneous?

- Did you go alone or with others?

- Did you buy anything?

- Did you enjoy it?

- What were your interactions with the salespeople like?

- Did you find that your moods were different before and after you shopped?

Helena, who lives on a fixed income and is slowly furnishing a new apartment, enjoys looking through favorite catalogues without any intention of buying. After a while she feels almost as if she has actually bought something. But when she feels down, she will occasionally on impulse call up a mail-order house and buy something that she would never otherwise order. A runny nose or an argument at work, combined with a silly blind date, will put her over that emotional limit toward a sofa bed she cannot afford, a sampler of chocolate-covered macadamia nuts, a CD recording of a favorite symphony that she already has on tape. When her impulsive purchase arrives, she feels foolish; sometimes she even returns it, at considerable inconvenience.

Valerie knows how to use shopping as a cure for depression without letting spending control her. She knows she need not actually buy much to elevate her mood—and she knows that the exploration of new clothing styles or just trying on a new outfit will make her feel much better about herself. She enjoys giving advice to other shoppers in shared dressing rooms and asking them their opinions of her own prospective purchases. Sometimes a single such interaction can turn around her whole day.

Rather than giving in to a vague fear and ineffective attempts to avoid an uncomfortable feeling, try now to

1. name your loneliness;

2. describe to yourself in your journal the context in which it tends to come over you;

3. identify the pattern you now have in dealing with it.

Elise graduated from college last year and is living on her own in an unfamiliar city. A junior reporter for a newspaper, she loves her work; she thrives on the pressure of unexpected assignments and irregular hours. She had expected to share her apartment with a friend from college, but after they moved in, her friend went home to look after her mother, who was in an auto accident. Elise is learning to shop and cook for one, to furnish her space from flea markets and discount stores. But there are moments, especially when she comes home tired and

full of her day's experiences, when the cozy apartment seems
to echo emptily. She feels nearly adult most of the time, but
at these times she wants to call home. She stops herself because she doesn't want her parents to be concerned, and she
turns to her hobby, calligraphy; a special small table with
brushes and ink is ready for her, and she calms and soothes
herself by the meditative concentration on each stroke. An
hour later she is much readier to call her parents for a heart-
to-heart that will not weigh on them, but bring them close, as
well as make Elise feel better.

REACHING OUT

Some of us handle loneliness by withdrawing, making no
telephone calls, seeing no movies, and rejecting contact. Leaving home even on an idle excuse can be a positive way of
reaching beyond this response to our loneliness. Going out lets
us connect with others on an informal level, and a friendly
interaction with a shopkeeper can give us the social energy to
make that telephone call or join the group that will bring us
new acquaintances.

Celia would go a long way toward changing her unhappy
situation if she could get out of the house more often. An
unwillingly retired English teacher, she tends to spend day
after day lightly sipping vodka while she reorganizes her ex-
tensive library. She speaks of missing her students and the
scheduled life, but she rejects every suggestion that she might
tutor or substitute. The only thing that seems to lift her spirits
is chance encounters with old colleagues and students, but she
is reluctant to make plans to see them: she feels she is no
longer part of their community and is afraid of being pitied.
The alcohol dims her loneliness and fogs her motivation to
reach out.

Janet, a lab technician, has been more successful at dealing
with her aloneness. Divorced after a marriage in which her life
revolved around her husband, she felt deeply lonely, especially

during dinner, which had always been an anchoring ritual during the marriage. The habit of socializing as a couple was hard to let go of, and she was uncomfortable and tense as the only unpartnered person at gatherings. Cooking was also a problem: meals seemed to have lost all the joy they had when they were a nurturing social ceremony. She knew that she was neglecting herself when she began to lose weight.

She decided that feeding and mothering herself would be an important beginning. She started by asking other single acquaintances out to dinner. Soon she began to give small dinner parties, applying her family skills to her solitary situation. It took her four years, but she now has a network of new friends. When she is alone at home today, she enjoys her solitude because she knows that she could arrange a potluck at a moment's notice.

If you are more reclusive than you wish, is there a lifelong pattern of imbalance between solitude and sociability? Or are you recovering from a crisis and giving yourself time to heal?

Here are some suggestions for manageable first steps:

a. If you want to go out but don't feel able to deal with other people, go for a drive or a walk, taking a route you rarely choose. Let your sense of exploration take you beyond your immediate preoccupations. Or go grocery shopping, look at furniture, or browse in a bookstore.

b. Treat yourself to a meal out or just a dessert or a coffee. Just being in a public place may help you feel better.

c. If you don't feel quite that isolated, call a friend to go out with: a walk, a museum, a meal, or a shopping trip. Or just call for a chat on the phone.

No matter how lonely you feel, go to work and to other structured activities; fulfill all your responsibilities. The act of doing so can be healing in itself. Allowing the time blocks of our lives to give way—skipping class, calling in sick, not showing up at a meeting—only deepens the sense of distance from the outside world. One of the functions of structured time is to allow us to fulfill our responsibilities regardless of a sudden wish for reclusiveness.

PETS

A precious way to reach out comes from our pets, who are responsive, nonjudgmental, and loving in ways in which we humans are incapable. For some of us, our pets become our families, rooting us to our homes and establishing our routines.

Bettina was a journalist and editor until her retirement. Never married, she lived a busy traveling life. Just before she retired, she noticed hand tremors and the beginnings of a lurch in her walk: Parkinson's disease. Of all the deprivations that followed, writing and typing became the most poignant loss. Her social energy drew inward, and she stopped making efforts toward friends. A veterinarian friend, alert to the therapeutic effect of animals on isolated or depressed people, suggested that Bettina might like a pet.

Meanwhile, at the animal clinic, a small kitten survived when her mother was killed by a car. This orange fuzzball rode around in the pockets of the veterinary staff for the first two months of his life. Tiny, but with a huge, fearless, and loving personality, he became a charismatic presence in the clinic, and Bettina's friend had to fend off many potential adopters to save him for Bettina. When they met, it was instant love. Bettina and the kitten are inseparable now, and his obvious dependence on her has, quite literally, changed the quality of her life. What he eats, where he sleeps, how he plays, have given a shape and organization to her day.

When we have sustained a loss, a pet can often be a healing bridge from the past to the future. Melinda's live-in boyfriend of six years recently broke up with her. At first she was incapacitated with grief, unable to eat or sleep in their bedroom. He had left her their dog, Bonny, a lively sheltie who was ever demanding of games and outings. Melinda spent long nights hugging Bonny and weeping into her silky fur, and Bonny, sensing a need for stillness, licked the tears.

As the months passed, Bonny's needs became the beginning of Melinda's return to living. Although she herself had little interest in food, Bonny needed to eat, so Melinda had to go out for dog food. Slowly, playing together came back, and Melinda laughed again. Used to being let into the bedroom, Bonny continued to bark at the door, mystified by Melinda's change of sleeping quarters. To please her, Melinda is gradually making peace with the room. Soon, she thinks she and Bonny will move back in.

Do you have a pet? If so, which of your needs are met in the relationship? Love? Physical warmth? Play? A sense of being needed? Communication? Intellectual stimulation? Ritual and routine?

If you do not have a pet, you may want to think about adopting one, considering carefully the differences needed in care and attention among dogs and cats, birds and fish. If you find it difficult to spend time alone, an animal could become one of your most rewarding friends.

LONELINESS IN THE PRESENCE OF OTHERS

Sometimes at parties, or at convivial dinners, we can experience a special, poignant loneliness: feeling isolated within the group. We struggle to manufacture conversation and a sense of connection. We are driven into inappropriate volubility or resigned silence. We try to comfort ourselves with the thought that we have freely chosen the observer role. We force ourselves not to be the first to leave.

Loneliness and Solitude

When Delia moved to a new state for a fine job opportunity in her banking firm, she chose to rent a house in the distant suburbs in order to be able to garden, hike, and let her two dogs run free. Settled in contentedly, she soon discovered that established local networks were very hard to break into. Although neighbors and storekeepers were courteous, she was clearly a curiosity, a city woman living in a house by herself. After some months, as the usually self-assured woman she is, Delia decided to go to an open meeting and "social" of the Friends of the Library. She was active in discussions and felt that people listened to her opinions with interest. But afterward, as people stood around with tea and doughnuts, she could not seem to find anyone to talk to. No one approached her, and every time she approached a group the conversation lapsed into awkward silence. Her confidence plummeted, and she slipped home, apparently unnoticed. She spent a bad, lonely night, fretting at having made the mistake of moving so far from the city. A few days later, however, a neighbor stopped her at the post office to thank her for her contribution to the library and ask her to make sure to come to the next meeting.

Delia risked loneliness and reached out to her new community in the best way she could find. The experience of being an outsider was one of the most painful social experiences of her life.

So, too, within a marriage the sense of isolation in the presence of a spouse can be deeply devastating. Becky was married right out of high school to her first boyfriend when neither of them was much more than a teenager. Now, twenty years later, he continues to carouse with his male friends after his pressured days as a car salesman, and weekends are full of sports and beer-drinking activities. Becky has little to do with her husband other than housekeeping and making his meals at whatever odd hours he comes home. He is often critical and contemptuous of her, and he shares almost none of her interests: they have disparate tastes, hobbies, and ways of spending time. The differences have immobilized them. Yet they never talk about separating or divorce. Becky cannot imagine life as a divorcée and all that the word implies. She is afraid that the loneliness beyond the loneliness she already feels might be even worse. She swings miserably between deciding to leave him and panic at the thought of being unable to find a job and living alone. However, now that she has two friends who are recently divorced, she is beginning to ask questions. Who suggested separating first? How did they tell their families? Were the children upset? What was it like coming home to an empty house? How did they find lawyers? She is listening and rehearsing.

Like Becky, many of us stay in stale relationships rather than risk loneliness. Yet the loneliest moments can be those of pretended connection and intimacy, when parts of the self float in disconnected isolation. Other women rush into inappropriate or destructive relationships because they are afraid to explore themselves while alone. They feel that that connection with another, even if it is a fleeting one founded on little depth, helps them deal with the time they spend by themselves. Perhaps one of the hardest tasks of all is to accept the reality of our human condition: we can share with others, form bonds with them, and have some of our needs for intimacy met, but ultimately we are alone. We must make peace with our solitariness.

If we have difficulty reaching serene and pleasurable solitude, we are like many but not all other women. However, we too can work toward successful solitude, learning to enjoy our own company. As we think now about how we balance our sociability and time by ourselves, and as we slowly recognize and experiment with the techniques we usually use to deal with our loneliness, we can begin to reshape the "free" time we have. Gradually we can learn to spend it not in flights from emptiness, but in activities that enrich us and make us feel content within ourselves.

□
MINITASKS

You may want to ask those who share your home for some additional solitary time and space as you explore some of the exercises in this chapter.

1 ▪ Sit or lie down for five minutes; become aware of being alone. Focus on the ideas, images, and feelings that come to you, even if they make you uncomfortable. Continue this every day for two weeks, concentrating on your reactions to unstructured time, including daydreams, fantasies, and the wish to end the five minutes or extend them.

2 ▪ Perform one short, solitary activity each day that you enjoy but don't often permit yourself because you see it as self-indulgent. Make time for it even if it interferes with plans that others may have for you, explaining gently but firmly that this is something you must do. Examples: stopping to watch children at the local playground; listening to a favorite piece of music; leaving work to walk around the block; crawling into bed in the middle of the day and closing your eyes for a few minutes; running your hand over the cherrywood table to feel the smooth grain; taking a very long hot bath. Try to stick to this for two weeks, noting in your journal how you respond.

3 ▪ Imagine now that your plans to spend the weekend with a friend or spouse have suddenly been canceled. You will be alone the whole time, and you can't go anywhere because you have no transportation. What would be your first response?

   ▪ Disappointment, of course, and then some alarm at what to do?

   ▪ Relief or excitement at the gift of time?

Now consider what your first impulses and actions would be. Do you think you would

- Call someone, reaching for contact?

- Get deeply involved with a project?

- Sit with yesterday's paper?

- Watch television?

- Plan dinner?

- Wash your hair?

- Listen to music?

- Exercise?

- Sink into lethargy?

Close your eyes and imagine how you would feel over the course of the day. See if you can chart, in your journal, a scenario for the whole weekend alone, including your likely spirits and state of mind.

4 · Look at the following descriptions of loneliness and solitude, and find yourself as you most often are when alone at this time in your life:

   a. mourning (aching for past relationships)

   b. isolated (missing active social contacts)

   c. alienated (lacking a sense of meaning in current contacts)

   d. alone and restless (searching for structured activity)

   e. busily alone and content (involved in projects)

   f. solitary (inwardly serene)

Note this in your journal, with the date of the observation.

5 · If you are living alone and tend to eat haphazardly, choose one afternoon or evening per week, no deviation permitted, to shop for nutritious food that you particularly like.

a. Plan your dinner.

b. Set the table with candles or a cloth napkin, whatever you usually do when expecting company.

c. Cook as if you expect a guest. (You do. She's yourself.) If you wish, make enough for a second or third meal, and prepare also a favorite standby like a pasta salad, stew, or whatever, so that your refrigerator looks friendly and inviting for several days.

d. Treat your dinner that night as a ritual.

You can be casual again for the next six days, but on that one evening make a compact to be your own host and guest. Stick to this program for two months, and see if the quality of your eating habits throughout the week changes.

6 ▪ If you feel timid about embarking on even a short excursion alone, here are some initial steps that may help you find greater freedom and independence:

a. Go for a walk in an unfamiliar place near home, such as a park you don't use or a church you have never visited.

b. Stay there for half an hour, observing the surroundings, the people, and, most important, yourself alone without an agenda other than passing these moments.

c. Record your experience and feelings about this.

7 ▪ Then go further afield, to a zoo, lake, or some other place that you usually visit with others. Pretend you are in a foreign country and observe the passing scene as though you were a total stranger. Be aware of any sense of uneasiness.

▪ Are you uncomfortable?

▪ Are you afraid?

- Are you restless?

- Are you imagining what other people are thinking about you?

- Have you become immersed in the experience?

- Are you enjoying it?

8 · On paper, or right here in the space provided, describe whether or not you usually enjoy the following solitary activities:

a. Daydreaming

b. Tinkering

c. Cooking

d. Walking

e. Reading

f. Listening to music

g. Going out to museums

h. Cleaning

i. Sewing

j. Big household projects

k. Other

If there are any that you do not usually do alone but think you might enjoy, make a point of trying them soon.

9 • Locate yourself on the following scale representing sociability:

a. I like to be alone most of the time.

b. I like to have company sometimes, but not too often.

c. I enjoy social interaction, but I like being alone just as much.

d. I'm a pretty social person, but I also like to be alone.

e. I hate being alone.

During your lifetime, have the preferences been the same? How are they met in your current life?

8· Renewing the Past: Relationships with Parents

Even while we speak, the hour passes.

OVID

AS WE RECONSIDER OUR PASTS AS A WAY OF SUMMONING UP OUR best and strongest selves for the future, we are drawn across a challenging and perhaps thorny threshold: the transformation of our relationship with our parents. Each major change in our lives causes a reciprocal change in theirs. We move away from home, and they deal with the empty nest; we marry, they become in-laws; we become parents, they grandparents, and for the first time we can imagine them clearly as parents to us in our own infancy. When we initiate change in the dance of authority and dependence at any of these points, the possibility emerges for new dialogues. Our thresholds, and theirs, are moments of opportunity for us to examine and correct the distortions of our child's eye and move toward acceptance and wisdom.

It is time to think again about the ghosts of the past: our family's dirty linen, the jealousies, the mistakes and misunderstandings, the issues never talked about. Perhaps it is too late to heal old wounds completely, but it is never too late to mend and make peace. Our relationships can even change, in our own minds, with those who have passed away.

The impetus toward new understanding, closeness, or reconciliation with our parents may be present at all times. But at times of crisis it may sometimes seem especially strong. Crisis may cause us to reevaluate the whole constellation of our lives, as it evokes our deepest fears of being abandoned, unloved, overwhelmed, or attacked. How we chart our way through may depend in part on how much understanding we have of the deepest, often unconscious feelings that are connected with our experiences in childhood. Our parents can help.

As our parents become older, we have less time left with them to change our relationships. Any unresolved emotional work in relation to them may haunt our lives after they are gone, and we may be left with deep feelings of regret at opportunities lost. Now, at the same time that we may be feeling a new urgency, they may be growing weaker, and we may be increasingly responsible for them and their lives. We may be able to help both ourselves and our parents out of destructive patterns that could not be changed when we were younger and less sure of ourselves.

A more profound accounting to ourselves of our life histories can give us a chance to make creative use of the past. When we tell people about our childhoods, we choose among the threads and people of our past in order to make a coherent story about ourselves. We were, perhaps, "my father's darling," "the little mother," "the waif," "the mediator," "the tomboy," or "the rebel." These self-descriptions are edited and simplified versions of complex lives. We were different people to different family members, and our roles and personalities shifted at different periods of our development.

Out of the vast tapestry of our particular family with its actual and mythic history, we weave powerful vignettes into a fabric of our own design. We repeat certain phrases: "It's my wanderer father coming out in me." "There have always been

entrepreneurs in my family." "My mother's people were po-
tato farmers from Poland." "We lost everything in the Depression." Then there are the exceptional people in our family
histories, whose stories and exploits are told through the generations. A great-grandfather was a train man on the western
railroads, an aunt was a Ziegfeld Follies girl, a tycoon great-
uncle lost it all in one generation, and a grandmother was sent
from Russia at the age of twelve to avoid a pogrom, because
she was the strongest and most resourceful. There are pieces of
family history that we value and those we would rather forget.
We have inherited talents—"a head for figures," "musicality
from my mother's side," or "a natural athletic ability." We
hold to such ideas as "My father's family is easygoing and my
mother's is business-oriented and aggressive," or "It just isn't
our family's style." As we get older, we become aware of the
less advertised family flaws, like alcoholism, violent temper, or
an inability to sustain a successful marriage. We have quiet
fears that these flaws may lie latent within us or our children.

As children we selected models from among these histories
and images and shaped our ideals from them. The closest role
models, our parents, are so deeply embedded in us that most of
us walk, gesture, speak, and think somewhat like them. Other
family members, as well as teachers, coaches, and friends,
formed a further network for identification and idealization.

- Who were your role models as a small child, negative
and positive?

- What about in early adolescence?

- What about as a teenager?

- What values that stayed with you did these people teach
you?

- How did knowing them make you imagine your own
future life?

Now, even in adulthood, we can make choices about which influences to pattern ourselves by. We can reject models that are no longer constructive and make new selections from among our ancestral figures. We can aim toward discarding useless interior baggage and making room for new self-descriptions and identities.

Sally's family owned a large discount fabric store, where both her parents, and later she and her two brothers, worked. Sally married young, and when she was divorced at thirty she reentered the family business. Although always clever and efficient in the store, her real love was expensive fine fabrics, which the store did not carry. After her sons were grown, she became increasingly bored at work, although she knew that her parents were happy that she had become so "practical." She kept remembering herself as a little girl, wrapping herself in remnants, dancing and spinning around the darkened store in gauze and chiffon.

She began to think a lot about her mother's aunt, a single, self-supporting watercolorist who had sometimes come into the store to paint freehand on cotton cloth. Sally had loved to sit on her lap as she swept huge washes of color across the damp fabric. Her parents' disapproval of the "irresponsible" aunt had restrained Sally, but she now recalled the thrill of this relationship as she struggled with the drabness of her daily life.

One day a woman came into the store with samples of fabrics of her own design. It turned out that she was a teacher at a textile institute not too far away. She told Sally about continuing education classes there, and Sally toyed with the idea of enrolling in an evening course in making batiks. Her parents were amused and condescending, critical of anything "frivolous" that did not contribute directly to the family business. But with a dawning realization that this might be the beginning of a major change in her life, Sally enrolled.

Now, years later, Sally has graduated from the institute and is apprenticed to a design house. She has almost no income, but she feels a joyous certainty that she is in the right place. Her parents have lost her as a partner in the store and are only slowly and grudgingly accepting her new direction. Despite all her attempts, they show no interest in her designs. Sally makes constant efforts to stay connected with her parents in other ways, and their relationship is slowly changing: "It takes time to get used to you now, dressed so fashionably," they say. Whenever Sally finds herself reverting to the "practical" mode her parents instilled in her, she consciously stops and reminds herself of her artistic aunt.

SOURCES OF CONFLICT

All of us have conflicts with our parents; pause now and reflect on some of the issues that seem to come up over and over again.

- Are the conflicts between you and your mother different from those between you and your father?

- Do the conflicts seem to become greater at certain times of the year?

- In certain situations?

- In certain settings?

- Have the main areas of conflict shifted over the course of your lives?

Perhaps the issues between you and your parents are included in some of the following common sources of parent-child conflict:

- the gap between our parents' expectations for us and the realities of our lives;

- differences in religious, ethical, or social mores, based

perhaps simply on the fact that we were born into different generations;

  ▪ communication gaps due to differences in social status, if we have become more educated or more successful than they (or less so);

  ▪ dependency or neediness on the part of either the parent or the child and the guilt of the other at being unable fully to respond;

  ▪ the tendency to revert to past patterns, as parents infantilize children and children find themselves slipping into reciprocal old habits.

As you identify some of the sources of conflict, you may also wish to ask yourself whether you have a sincere wish to try to resolve the issues. Which would you most like to try to work on? Make a commitment, now, to experiment with new approaches to old problems, starting small, with a manageable goal in mind.

STRATEGIES

During childhood and adolescence, Liz's friends envied her for her charismatic and generous mother, Katherine. Liz's family was often larger by one or two children because friends sought refuge from their own stricter families in Katherine's open warmth. Katherine was always a center of activity: she organized games, fixed hurts, repaired torn clothes; she could knit you a sweater in her spare time. During the 1960s, when most of Liz's friends were fighting with their parents over drugs and sex, Katherine's household was a haven of permissiveness. The cautions of Liz's more conservative father seemed merely negative and weak next to Katherine's powerful positive energy. Everyone told Liz that she was lucky.

Yet to Liz it seemed that Katherine shone the same warmth

on almost everybody without discrimination; there seemed little difference between Katherine's feelings for Liz and her feelings for Liz's friends. The world revolved around Katherine's sun, and Liz felt left on the side, watching.

During her adolescence, Liz berated herself for her own unhappiness: her mother was "an amazing woman"—so why did she feel so empty? Continuously disappointed and hurt at home, she successfully lobbied her parents to send her to boarding school for a year in Europe.

Liz cut off almost all contact with her mother during her college years; a phone call, which rarely came, could upset her for days. She threw her search for love into her boyfriends and into her achievements as an outstanding student, competitive ice skater, and overall superwoman.

Through therapy, and through conversations with her father, who deeply admired Katherine but had finally given up on an emotionally one-sided marriage, Liz began to understand that there was a good reason for her own neediness. Katherine herself had been so emotionally bruised in childhood that she had formed a shell around herself, learning to be almost completely emotionally self-sufficient. One of her great sources of power and appeal was her independence and lack of need for others; her warmth toward others was in many ways transitory. Having children had been a project that she had thrown herself into, then tired of as her attention was drawn to other areas.

Liz found she was happier after she stopped looking for something from Katherine that she was unable to give. Yet Liz's entire life was colored by a search. Sometimes she was able to find someone to give her a sense of being loved and needed; but because she was often attracted to emotionally distant people who reminded her unconsciously of her mother, she was also often hurt.

Then, when Liz was in her thirties, happily married to a man who understood her well and could meet most of her needs, she began to find it easier to be with Katherine. This was in part because Katherine herself had changed: after the divorce she seemed to have an increased awareness of her own frailties and to need her children more. Furthermore, by going to work as a buyer for a gourmet food store, she was able to pursue an interest she had put on hold while she was meeting the demands of being a mother.

Then came a threshold for Katherine and Liz: deeply troubled by her impending retirement and the prospect of having time on her hands, Katherine told Liz of her dreams of starting a small home bakery. Liz, who now had plenty of cash in the bank, saw that she should step in and help. She offered to put up the start-up money and become her mother's backer. Katherine accepted joyfully.

To Liz's amazement, the project became the grounds for a reconciliation that had eluded them for more than twenty years. At last Katherine needed her, not only for financial support, but also for her expertise in arranging for contractors for the new kitchen, for publicity and marketing, and for many other details the two of them had decided to handle on their own. Katherine telephoned her frequently to share worries. Liz was touched to discover that when she was unable to get away for the weekend, Katherine was sincerely disappointed. Liz began to see her mother as a person who did in fact have needs, whether or not she could admit them to herself, and that in her own way her mother was being, and had been, as good a mother as she knew how.

Liz tried a variety of strategies for changing her relationship with her mother before she arrived at the present happy solution. We can consider now whether they would help us to improve our own situations:

a. *Changing our own behavior* and refusing to participate in entrenched, mutually destructive patterns.

b. *Changing our own expectations* so that we forgive our parents and are no longer surprised or hurt by them.

c. *Developing new mutual activities and finding new settings* so that we can explore, through deed rather than word, new ways of relating to one another.

d. *Actively intervening* with aging or distressed parents, helping to arrange new life solutions for them.

e. *Moving away or removing ourselves* from the parental orbit, if the relationship between ourselves and our parents is irredeemably destructive or stagnant.

As a young teenager Liz had tried to stop participating in destructive patterns by talking with her mother about what she needed; when that did not work, she moved away from home and tried complete avoidance. For Liz, the strategies that worked best were reducing her expectations by accepting her mother's limitations and finding new mutual activities. Active intervention in helping her mother as she aged also gave Liz a new sense of confidence and power in a relationship in which she had often felt helpless. Consider now, in greater detail, the stories of women who used each of these five strategies, to see if they point you toward tools for changing your own relationships with your parents.

CHANGING OUR OWN BEHAVIOR

Grace, a widow of sixty, made the first strategy work for her. She was the sole member of her family left to care for her eighty-two-year-old mother, Charlotte, a matriarch who continued to live alone in the rambling Victorian house that had been the family home for seven children, assorted aunts, and servants. Always a person of conviction and power, Charlotte presided like a queen over the empty house, refusing to move even though there were times when her increasing blindness and forgetfulness could have been dangerous. All her dynastic power became concentrated on Grace, from whom she demanded absolute obedience, precision in visiting hours, shopping, and cooking. She was critical of all of Grace's efforts to allow other helpers in the house, even to shop or clean. No one was ever thorough enough.

Grace was wilting under this barrage of emotional demands. Finally she went to see a woman therapist, who helped her unravel a childhood history in which Grace had been singled out for punishment whenever any of the children grew rowdy. She began to understand that she had always been afraid of her mother. By admitting her resentment and recalling memories of hurt and longing, Grace realized that she had never been able to set limits on her mother's demands. Instead she had been endlessly responsive in the forlorn hope of winning approval.

Fortified by her insight, Grace gently began to establish new boundaries between herself and Charlotte. At first she changed minor things: she said she couldn't come at ten o'clock, but she would be free by lunch; that she could take her mother to the hairdresser not immediately, as asked, but the next day. Charlotte stormed, sensing Grace's new independence. There was a long battle of wills, and Grace was not always able to stand up to her. At last, however, Grace went on her first vacation away from her mother in years, hiring a live-in caregiver over Charlotte's violent objections.

On her return, to her great surprise, she learned that her mother had made peace with the caregiver and actually wished to continue the new situation. Although Grace recognized that this was, in part, a prideful rejection, she felt that her insistence on doing things differently had helped both of them find a way out of ancient patterns. As her mother became less demanding, Grace came to look forward to finding new ways of making her mother more contented.

Changing our own behavior by using the element of surprise can be an important ally for us. Well-timed anger or playfulness can sometimes shock others into understanding what might otherwise elude them.

Adrianna, a lawyer nearing fifty, is Faith's only child.

Mother and daughter have always considered themselves very close. Then, when Faith was seventy, she was widowed. She seemed to blame the world for her misery. She lashed out at Adrianna when they saw each other; she made distraught, reproachful phone calls apparently intended to make Adrianna feel responsible for her situation. Finally Adrianna grew impatient with her mother's self-pity and angry at the change in their long, supportive relationship.

One memorable night Adrianna lost her temper and told her mother that she was destroying any semblance of affection between them. She left the house, leaving her mother in tears. Faith spent a sleepless night and, exhausted, telephoned Adrianna in the morning. Adrianna came over, and they had their first real talk in years. Adrianna realizes now that her outburst might have had disastrous consequences, pushing her mother even deeper into depression. But she felt that she had to do something drastic to cut through the distance between them. Today Faith is living near Adrianna. She will never be truly comfortable living alone, but she has grudgingly accepted the situation and gets a deep, protective joy from her relationship with her daughter.

By contrast, Patty used not anger but playfulness and humor as tools to shake her mother into greater awareness. From the time Patty was small, her mother had always emphasized her disapproval by shaking a critical finger close to Patty's face. Even when Patty was in her thirties, her mother continued to use the old gesture. One day, exasperated but also amused, Patty grabbed hold of her mother's upraised finger, shook a reproachful finger in her mother's face, and said, "Do you know that you've been doing this all my life?" Her mother was genuinely mortified and said that she was not even aware of the mannerism. The next time she found herself shaking her finger, she grabbed hold of it herself and said, "No more of that from you from now on." Mother and daughter both had a good laugh. The now somewhat infirm mother was no longer in a position to wield power and criticism; Patty was no longer in awe or frightened of her mother's disapproval. The affection between them had been preserved, however, through the transition.

- If you have ever tried to change your relationships with your parents by setting new boundaries, how have they reacted?

- Have they ever tried to set new boundaries with you?

- If so, how did that make you feel?

- Have you ever used anger as an effective tool for changing your relationships with your parents?

- What about humor?

Consider now an area in which you would like to make some relatively minor change in your interactions with one or both of your parents, and experiment with changing your habitual behavior as a way of carving out new paths with them. If they ask, tell them honestly why you are trying out a new pattern.

CHANGING OUR OWN EXPECTATIONS

Sometimes we solve the problem simply by accepting our parents for what they are, forgiving them for their limitations, and perhaps even finding some lovableness in their predictability. They can no longer hurt us when we can say, perhaps with weary amusement, "That's just the way Dad is."

Sandy hated to go home from college for holidays. While in school, she felt like a responsible adult, in control of her feelings and her use of time. But the minute she came in the front door at home, the politics of family life were what they had always been, and Sandy felt like an embattled and invaded twelve-year-old. If she tried to help out in the kitchen, her mother criticized her for drying the glasses wrong; if she turned on the television, her father wanted to change the channel, even though he hadn't been watching in the first place. Nothing she could do was right; it was a rare holiday that passed without tears and the resolution never to come again.

During Sandy's junior year, she took a psychology course in interpersonal dynamics. She reflected on the hidden meaning of the inharmonious, infantilizing dialogue that plagued her family life. Sandy began to understand the interaction from her parents' side as well as her own and to see in their intrusiveness a concern and attempt to control a child they no longer knew.

Sandy began to telephone them more often and keep them abreast of what her life was like, in an attempt to make them feel included and alleviate their worries. She also decided that the next visit home would be short. Because she knew that outsiders can sometimes provide buffers and make families behave better, she brought along a girlfriend. When they arrived, her parents showered Sandy with the familiar, intrusive concern and rule making, but she did not take the bait and quietly changed the subject, asking them about their lives. Whenever they got on her nerves she took her girlfriend out on a walk. Without explaining or confronting them, she allowed her parents to be what they needed to be: anxious parents reacting with anguish to the empty nest.

- What characteristics of each of your parents most hurt, concern, or irritate you?

- Do you think they will ever be able to change?

- Do you think you might be able to make things easier for yourself if you could simply accept and forgive them for these things?

Now identify one minor area in which one or both parents irritate or hurt you. Work on your own attitudes, so that the next time you find yourself reacting to this behavior, you mentally shrug your shoulders and simply acknowledge to yourself that this is the way they are. Remind yourself that their behavior is not your responsibility.

DEVELOPING NEW MUTUAL ACTIVITIES

An effective way of breaking out of old patterns of interaction lies in trying out new activities or settings. We may, for example, travel or embark on a project with a parent or have Thanksgiving at our house instead of theirs. Habits change quickly when different facets of our personalities come to the fore; in a new environment we have different roles that force us to relate to one another differently. The results can be surprisingly gratifying.

Aida, a high school biology teacher in a big urban public school, lives a thousand miles from her small-town parents. Visits in either direction had become less and less frequent, partly because her parents were disappointed that Aida had remained single and partly because visits to the big city were stressful for them and going home was dull for her. When her mother developed a serious kidney infection, Aida realized with some shock that they had grown very far apart.

As she visited her mother in the hospital during her recovery, she proposed that the three of them travel together the following summer. She suggested going to the Salzburg Music Festival, a yearly event that they had all read and dreamed about for many years. After much excited discussion, they agreed that they could afford to go. Aida made the arrangements. For a week, in a glorious setting, the three of them enjoyed concert after concert and in the process rediscovered each other, not as parents and child, but as adults having one of the most memorable times of their lives.

- Are there certain settings in which your relationship with your parents is more likely to revert to destructive ancient patterns?

- When did you last go to a neutral place with them?

- How was it different from being on their territory or yours?

- When did you last do something out of the ordinary with your parents?

- Are there activities that you and they once shared that you have not done together in many years?

The next time you discuss getting together, consider whether you would like to meet in a new place or do something you have never done together or have not done in many years. There is no need to make a big deal out of this: approach the excursion in the spirit of fun and openness to whatever may emerge from it.

ACTIVELY INTERVENING

When our parents age, we often reenter their lives in a new way. Three out of every four of us will be active caregivers to one or both parents at some time. It may feel as if the walls of domestic responsibility are closing in again just when we felt we wanted to try new things. We help to support them by visiting, cooking, having them live with us, or making that wrenching decision to arrange for a nursing home. The challenge for us is to deal with this caretaking so that it is not a burden but an opportunity.

There is usually a slow and painful passage from total ignorance about the practical side of caring for a parent to knowledge, skill, and acceptance of a whole new way of being together. As we may once have struggled with a whole new world by becoming a parent, it can seem strange and frightening to learn to become the parent of our parent. We are handicapped here by our own anxiety about aging and death. It can be deeply unsettling and threatening to watch a parent whom we have known to be more capable and stronger than ourselves gradually weaken, becoming ill and dependent. For a long time daughter and parent may pretend, denying change and holding on to older roles.

Ann-Marie's mother, who is sixty-eight, lives in a small apartment near Ann-Marie. She has lived there alone for the last twenty years, since she was widowed, fiercely guarding her independence. Until recently she was driving competently and, to all outward appearances, "aging well." But Ann-Marie noticed that her mother was making excuses to avoid driving at night and then driving less often during the day. Ann-Marie knew too that her mother was hiding a minor loss of bladder control, secretly buying minipads. Also, Ann-Marie noticed that she had stopped buying canned goods, as they became too difficult for her arthritic hands to open. Mother and daughter allowed these small signs to go unmentioned to preserve the mother's dignity and pride. But the mutual denial slowly created a gulf between them. Spontaneity died.

One day Ann-Marie noticed a pair of waterproof panties soaking in the bathroom sink and could no longer go on pretending. Her mother was deeply embarrassed, but she admitted that she had had a problem with this for several years. Almost immediately she felt glad to be able to share the maneuvers she had invented in order to conceal various other new weaknesses. She had learned to drink less water before bedtime and sleep downstairs where the bathroom was closer; she had manufactured reasons to ask friends for rides, hiding her anxiety about her deteriorating sight. Mother and daughter managed to have a good, comforting talk about their mutual deviousness and went out to celebrate their new honesty by buying an electric can opener.

Once her mother's needs were open for discussion, Ann-Marie found she enjoyed being helpful when asked. She invited her mother to move in with her family, but her mother said that she valued living separately and found it an interesting challenge to work out how to do tasks that had once been so easy. But the idea of moving had been broached, and she knew that Ann-Marie cared and was ready. Together the two of them began to anticipate the need for outside help, investigating resources, costs, and eligibility requirements. Ann-Marie's mother had matured in that she was now able to stop denying her needs and accept help; Ann-Marie had matured in that she could give help without fearing that her mother would try to control her.

If you come away from caring for a dependent parent feeling exhausted and trapped, it is time to look in the telephone book, usually at the beginning or in the last few pages, for a section called "Community Services." Look for the subheading "Aged" or "Elderly." Here you will find councils for the elderly, homemaker services, elderly day care, Meals on Wheels, visiting nursing services, senior transport services, and more. There is a gold mine of free or low-fee services that you can slowly introduce into your lives, making coexistence possible and avoiding or delaying the need for nursing-home care. There is help for you, too. Look for support groups for Alzheimer family members, hospices for families of the dying, and many others.

- Have you ever had to intervene in the lives of your parents when they were in trouble?

- If so, how did that change the dance of dependency and authority between you?

- Do either of or both your parents have major problems, such as alcoholism, poor health, or desperate loneliness, that you or they may be ignoring or denying?

This latter could, of course, have serious consequences. The desire for autonomy quite often leads aging parents, like Ann-Marie's mother, to conceal and deny, vehemently hanging on to solitary living. Then suddenly a fall, a fire, or confusion at the bank reveals the chaos and the danger. There is the shock of recognition by the family that help has been too little and too late; there is no longer an opportunity for gradual working toward dependence without loss of pride. This can end in a precipitous move to a nursing home, with resentment, guilt, and depression on both sides. Sometimes a stubborn clinging to self-sufficiency may even make intervention impossible.

Eleanor's parents, Robert and Elsie, owned and operated a ski lodge following Robert's retirement at sixty. Ten years later Elsie broke her hip in a car accident and was confined to a wheelchair. They sold their inn and distributed or sold their huge houseful of fine furniture and other possessions, moving into a small, wheelchair-accessible apartment. Robert learned to shop, cook, and do errands but never very well. Visiting children tried to help, but Robert refused angrily. As he became more and more absentminded, the apartment became chaotic and meals haphazard.

Although they had refused Eleanor's offer to have them move in with her, they agreed to look into retirement communities. They often found long waiting lists. Some were unwilling to accept someone in a wheelchair; others were prohibitively expensive. Elsie and Robert rejected nursing homes as being for people more frail and disorganized then they felt they were. Finally they found a boarding house with wheelchair-accessible bathrooms and handholds everywhere. It provided three meals a day, laundry services, and nursing supervision. Robert and Elsie felt that here they would still be able to have the self-respect and independence that were so important to them. Once again, furniture and belongings were sorted and redistributed. Only the antique maple spindle bed, theirs during sixty years of marriage, remained with them. Although they were given a sunny first-floor room, they complained about the food and the regulated mealtimes. A crisis developed when, against the recommendations of the live-in nursing staff, Robert rebelliously drove to town to buy a newspaper and got lost. During the frantic half-day search for him (he turned up in a gas station an hour's drive away), Elsie had a stroke. She died in the hospital soon after. Disoriented, bereft, and agitated, Robert too had to be hospitalized. He faded away and died in less than a year.

Although the end might have been the same had her parents consented to live with her, Eleanor is still sad that she could not ease those last months for them, and she often imagines, fruitlessly, how things might have been different if she had somehow convinced them of their welcome. She is angry, too, that their stubbornness and inability to accept their own changed situations kept them from turning to the family for help. She is working on forgiving herself, and them, for their rejection of her.

So, too, we need to forgive ourselves when we are unable to do everything we would have liked for our parents. Although they may be weaker and frailer than they once were, they are still adults, and they alone bear ultimate responsibility for their lives.

MOVING AWAY OR REMOVING OURSELVES

Avoidance of contact may be the solution of last resort for some daughters. Sometimes, to protect our growth or psychological well-being, we must move away from the parental orbit. This may mean reducing time together or, sadly, it may be necessary to cut off all contact, perhaps moving to another community, separating ourselves from their influence and the power that they wield.

It was clear to Patrice, who was adopted six months prior to the unexpected birth of another daughter, that from babyhood she had been a disappointment. She was not a "real" daughter; she was clumsy and "bad," not feminine and delicate like her sister and her mother. Retreating into books and study, she built self-confidence in the only area in which she seemed to have some success—her mind. She was nicknamed "the family brain," but there was no love or pride in this name.

In college, where she paid her own way, and later as a graduate student and then as a research scientist, she mended her self-image. But a visit home could rip it to shreds. Her mother's condescending laughter—"Still watching beetles for a living?"—cut deep. Patrice, usually verbal and witty among her friends, was always reduced to silence. Once, in a last desperate attempt to make her mother understand, love, and respect her, she tried to talk about her pleasure in her work; slightly drunk, her mother called her a "whore intellectual." That was the last time Patrice went home. Her sister understands. She winced all her life as she watched Patrice's emotional massacre, sometimes trying without success to intercede on her behalf.

Life has been better for Patrice, and in some ways for the whole family, since she let go of her hopes and removed herself from the hurtful environment. She still hopes that someday her parents may see that it was not her fault that she came into their lives under the circumstances that she did. But for now, however temporarily, she would rather try to create her own new family network.

- Have there been times in your life when you and your parents ceased communicating?

- If so, what was that like for each of you?

- Did your experiences and growth during the separation better prepare you for dealing with your parents when you resumed contact?

Although there may be times when we need to be totally cut off from our parents, these times need not last forever. Our journey together is a long one, and just as the closest bonds may be ruptured, so may the deepest rifts be repaired. Like us, our parents are changing constantly, and the roles they hope we will play in their lives shift accordingly. Patience, forgiveness, and a sense of history and possibility will help to guide us, no matter how frequently or infrequently we actually speak or see each other.

All of these women were able, however slightly, to shift the configuration between themselves and their parent(s). In the delicate negotiation toward becoming less a daughter and more a friend and helper, anger, laughter, and gentle and not-so-gentle self-assertion all have a place. All daughter-parent pairs will traverse the emotional landscape of separation and reunion uniquely, depending upon the particular balance of personalities, style of family communication, and shared history. But traverse it we all do and must, with many stages and variations over the course of our lives. The task is to build ties that give us joy and a sense of continuity and to enhance our own and our parents' growth in the process.

It is time now to reflect on the familial ground out of which we were formed, lineage, traits, flaws, and all. By doing so, we may arrive clear of mind at our current juncture. We may accept the strengths of our relationships with our parents as supports for the next stretch, while looking more closely at the less positive aspects, so that if these hold us back today, we can work on containing or changing them.

□

MINITASKS

You may want to use your journal (if you are keeping one) to record your thoughts as you consider the issues raised by some of the minitasks in this chapter. Remember to allow yourself enough time to really think about some of these minitasks; don't try doing too many at once!

1 ▪ Name one positive trait that your family felt you had that was important in your childhood.

- How did you feel about it?

- Did you try to live up to it?

- Was it a source of pride?

- Was it a source of pressure?

- To what extent does this description continue to affect your relationships to your parents today?

The next time you see your parents, discuss this image and tell them how it has shaped you and your self-image.

2 ▪ Now name one negative trait that your family felt you had that was important in your childhood.

- Did you feel it was true?

- Were you hurt or angry about it?

- Did you try to prove them wrong?

- Does this description still affect your self-image?

- Do your parents still feel this way about you?

- If so, does it affect your relationship with them?

The next time you see them, talk about this old stereotype and discuss how it came into being.

3 ▪ Some time when you have just left a visit with your parent(s) and are feeling angry, exhausted, disappointed, or sad, write down the characteristics that aggravate or bother you at this moment, on this particular day. You may feel, for example, that he or she was controlling, self-pitying, helpless, insensitive, or demanding.

Then write down your own typical response to these characteristics: for example, subservience, rage, resentment, pity, or irritation. This exercise may help you to be clearer about the emotional dance between you.

Finally, consider your early experience to see if this is a lifelong pattern or one that has been recently activated or accentuated by some change in circumstances.

4 ▪ Describe in your journal one point of irritation or tension between yourself and one of your parents. For example: their intrusiveness, forgetfulness, rigidity, criticism of the way you raise your children, disapproval of your life-style or partner, and so on.

Which of the five strategies have you tried in dealing with this problem?

a. Refusing to participate in old behavior patterns;

b. Lowering your expectations;

c. Actively intervening on your parent's behalf;

d. Finding new projects or activities to share;

e. Avoiding the parent entirely.

The next time you see or telephone that parent, try one of the strategies you have not used and write down the results in your journal.

5 ▪ Now repeat this exercise with the other parent.

6 ▪ For each of the five strategies, write down one situation in which you have used it with each of your parents.

- Which one have you used most often?

- Which has been most effective?

7 ▪ Imagine that your parents invite you to travel with them for a week, to do something that you would enjoy. What would be your reaction?

I would refuse because

a. I would be continuously miserable.

b. Our relationship is too fragile to spend that much time together.

c. They would only want me to be there to help them with their travel arrangements.

d. They would be trying to expiate guilt toward me, and I don't want to participate.

e. Other.

I would go, cautiously, because

a. I would like to use the time to try to know them in a new way.

b. They need me, and it is only fair that I help them enjoy themselves.

c. I love them, and it is my duty to try to make them happy.

d. Other.

I would go enthusiastically.

8 ▪ Name five turning points in your life, and name the reciprocal ones in the lives of your parents, if any. For example:

Going to nursery school/Change in parenting role; Moving away from home/Dealing with an empty nest; Getting married/ Becoming in-laws; and so forth.

Myself	My parents
1.	1.
2.	2.
3.	3.
4.	4.
5.	5.

9 ▪ Now do the same for five turning points in each of their lives, naming how these changes have affected you. For example: Going back to work/Feeling a little abandoned now that Mommy expects you to be a grown-up; Remarrying/ Dealing with a stepparent; Becoming a widow or widower or retiring/Taking more responsibility for them.

My Mother	Myself
1.	1.
2.	2.
3.	3.
4.	4.
5.	5.

My Father	Myself
1.	1.
2.	2.
3.	3.
4.	4.
5.	5.

10 ▪ When parents or a group of other family members are gathered together, perhaps at Thanksgiving or Christmas, tape a huge piece of brown wrapping paper onto the wall. Together, write a family tree, to see what knowledge you have in common and where the gaps are. The eldest people present will become the experts, and one of them may be a self-appointed historian. Elicit as much as possible from the anecdotes about Great-Uncle Steve and his travels, Aunt Lucy's gift for poetry, and so on. Keep the tree, and extend and elaborate on the personalities, updating and adding when different family members are present.

11 ▪ At a family gathering talk about past rituals such as Thanksgivings or ancestral immigrations. Tape the conversations, if people feel comfortable about it. If this proves interesting, repeat it, refining family knowledge with other relatives. Include the youngest ones; ultimately, the stored family knowledge will be for them.

12 ▪ Take out old photograph albums and look through the earliest ones slowly with an older relative, your mother or grandmother, for example. Learn as much as you can about her as a child, adolescent, young woman, young married, or young parent. How did she get along with her parents? What was her family role vis-à-vis her siblings? Pay attention to what her order of birth was and what siblings were most important to her. Tell her as clearly as you can how important it is to you to know exactly how life was for her then.

13 ▪ Begin a conversation with a parent around a photograph of a person important in the past, such as your grandmother, a dead father, your long-absent sister. Ask for early memories, and listen carefully. Don't ask for logical sequences or time dates; just listen. Tape-record the memories, if doing so enhances the teller's sense of the importance of the ritual.

14 • Take out a baby and child album and listen to your mother's or father's version of you and your place in the family, including your characteristics then, as they saw them. Make this a way of talking about your shared pasts, and suggest that you are different now and can carve out new ways of being together. If it has been a difficult relationship, talk openly about whatever strengths you give your parent(s) credit for; if it has been very close and even, with the areas of conflict suppressed or ignored, try to bring the conversation to a deeper level of truthfulness.

9 · Relationships: Lovers and Friends

I hold this to be the highest task of a bond
between two people: that each should stand
guard over the solitude of the other.

RAINER MARIA RILKE

AS WE PASS OVER A NEW THRESHOLD DOWN A NEW PATH, WE AF-
fect or even shake the people central to our lives. The shift
from inertia to motion in part of any network creates change in
the whole, however small. Our changes reverberate to all of
our partnerships: lovers and husbands, friends, and even pets.
Our concern for them is thus included in our own transformation. We invite you now to explore ways of making these
important existing relationships more vital, as well as to consider strategies for creating new friendships that may enrich
your life in new ways.

LOVERS AND HUSBANDS

Long-term partnerships offer us many rewards. The first and
most obvious is companionship. Having someone to come
home to after a long day, or waiting for someone to come
home, is a reminder of our strong connection to another,

someone with whom we can share our experiences. When we are reunited after our brief separations, the small pleasures, annoyances, and surprises of the day fall into perspective. Together with another warm and active person, we have for years or decades been building a nest. We know that it is safe to rely on our partner; it makes us happy to be needed in return.

The second is that our sexual needs are more or less satisfied, predictably and securely. As single and divorced people know, the search for a sexual partner can be a miserable and frustrating experience. AIDS and herpes further dampen our enthusiasm for taking on new partners.

The third, most profound gift of a long-term relationship is that we are witnesses to each other's journeys through time. We show each other our connections to the past and our paths toward the future. Above all others, we have been witnesses to each other's growth and change. Our partner has known us, perhaps, as a woman who was his date, then his bride, then the mother of his child; he has seen us, perhaps, get a new job, earn a promotion, have a fight with our boss. He knows our many facets and moods: as a loving person mourning the death of a grandmother or a pet, as a happy person laughing with a friend, as a relaxed person reading on the beach or enjoying a fine meal. Our shared rituals give us a sense of security; our daily repetitions teach us the beauty of orderly ordinariness. Together we have created our own language of gestures and signals. Our lives wind through time and space, touching, turning, separating only to touch again; we know and are known.

Two people do not necessarily grow and change in the same direction; either one may change in ways that exclude the other. In some of the more common scenarios, men may seek affairs or pursue ever more demanding careers, while women are left behind to tend the nest or a lesser career. There is also the opposite pattern, with men unwilling or unable to make radical changes, their roles as breadwinners deeply connected with their sense of responsibility as husbands and fathers, while women continue to experiment and explore.

In general, we women can more easily imagine ourselves in changed situations. Most of us once were childless, then passed dramatically into mothering and then into the balancing act between parenting and work. Changes in children's needs echoed into our home and work life. We retire not only once but many times. We are typically in and out of the work place in response to husbands' relocations, new babies, the need to make more money suddenly, career changes, or illnesses. We bend with the wind and have confidence that in our bending we do not break. Compromise is an old friend.

Now we may want to sort out what our partner can and cannot be for us or to consider ways in which to enrich our relationship with him. We may be exploring new areas where sharing is not possible or even desirable. Our partner may applaud our growth, feel enriched by it, or feel freed by it to begin changes of his own. He may also feel abandoned or surpassed, or discouraged because he can't find the thread of change in himself. He may require care, patience, and humor as we think and read deeply for the first time in years, become fit, or travel more adventurously to places where he may follow only reluctantly or not at all. Any long-term partnership involves recognition of deep differences and acceptance of equally deep compromises. We talk about the night owl versus the early bird, the delicate eater versus the gourmand, the cautious tourist versus the impulsive traveler, the deliberate, slow-paced planner versus the high-energy firebrand. By identifying such sources of tension or difference, we can feel less vulnerable, upset, or puzzled when we clash.

Habits of feeling, communication, and daily activities are comforting in their predictability. But if they have become stifling or joyless for you, or if the relationship is causing you pain, you will want to consider how to break out of these cycles. Perhaps neither partner can imagine breaking away, fearing dislocation, financial hardship, and disruptions that may extend far beyond the family and call into question many roles and commitments. Even a stale relationship may have its rewards: continuity, security, and depth, reinforced by social networks and perhaps some mutual permission to have some intellectual, social, or even sexual needs met by other people, may help to sustain it.

Never assume you know your partner fully: just as you have facets of personality never expressed when you are with him, so he too is many people, of whom you know only some. Whether considering the drastic decision to separate or simply wanting to change your relationship for the better, you may begin by considering the following strategies:

a. Perhaps you both need to do separately what you once did together.

b. Or you may need to explore joining one another in what you each once did alone.

c. Or you may find new projects to share, an adventure for both.

Letting go can often be the best medicine for a troubled relationship. Jerry and Susan's marriage was imperiled: both felt that the joy had gone out of life. Neither could remember the last time they had done anything new or exciting, but they couldn't seem to break out of old habits. They had rented the same lakeside cottage for their two-week summer vacation for the past ten years.

Then, the summer their son turned thirteen, he went off to camp. A friend of Jerry's asked him to go with him on a trip across country. This had no appeal for Susan, who wanted to take an intensive computer course to upgrade her position at work. With the frank understanding that this would give them a chance to think things over and reevaluate the marriage, they decided to forgo the cottage and go their separate ways. But the longer they were apart, the more they missed each other; they returned to each other with a new appreciation of the marriage and of each other.

David and Frances had very different styles of spending leisure time. David was sedentary and intellectual, Frances physical and artistic. As they reached the end of their first decade together, they seemed to have become even more intensely typecast in this way, spending more and more time apart. Discussing this one day, they agreed that each would try actively participating in one of the other's interests for a trial period.

This worked out surprisingly well. David now plays a fair game of tennis and has become an avid Wimbledon fan; Frances has gone to many more movies with David and joined him in his interest in the history of film. They often rent classics from the video store, reading about them first and then discussing them together.

Jim and Rachel are city folk, neither one particularly handy. When their two sons were in their teens, Jim inherited a piece of land from his grandmother. Although they had talked of having a country house, neither had ever done anything about this not-very-serious dream. Going to look at the land, the whole family became excited, together choosing the best site on the lot for a cabin.

They spent July taking a course in building. In August, on the strength of that, they and the boys put up a prefabricated cabin. There were squabbles and errors, but even more shared delight.

Think now about the things you and your partner do together and about the things you do alone.

- What would it be like to do separately one of the things you now do together?

- What would it be like to try to share with your partner something that you usually do alone?

- Is there anything that he usually does alone that you could imagine doing with him?

- Now consider ideas you have had of things to do together that you have never acted upon. Which of these would be easiest to try?

Be sure to start small, with manageable steps, and to discuss your plans with your partner. Small changes in behavior may also lead to clearer communication about larger areas of concern, or dreams or desires you may have for the relationship. Take the case of Susan, a botanist by training, who had always wanted to plant a large garden. When she and her husband, Richard, finally had the means to buy a country home on a five-acre lot, they decided to cultivate the garden together. This step was risky for Susan, because Richard, a business-man, had a strong need to be in control. Usually this led Susan to spend much of her leisure time pursuing her own projects, lest she feel like Richard's employee. Predictably Richard began telling Susan how they were going to proceed with the planting, ignoring her expertise and experience. Susan calmly pointed out that since she had the training in this area, perhaps this was a situation in which she should be the boss. Although it was very difficult for Richard, he was able to subsume his need for control while they planted and took care of the garden.

The experience was a turning point in their marriage. Not only were they able to enjoy the fruits of their labor, but the garden provided them with the opportunity to discuss Rich-ard's need for control, which had so often spoiled the little free time they had shared together in the past. Now Susan and Richard are finding more ways to share activities and are finding that they enjoy each other's company more than they have in years.

Susan and Richard's experience shows how we can ease slowly into significant changes in our relationships. By sharing activities that foster communication, we can change our patterns without creating trauma or threatening our partner into rigidity. Remember to be flexible and to tread softly, feeling your way into a new balance in the relationship and thus creating a new dance for the two of you. Of course, your best efforts may also prove futile, showing you that it is time to end the relationship.

NEW RELATIONSHIPS

If we are without a committed partner for the first time in a while, we may feel that our universe has temporarily collapsed. We will probably feel somewhat uncertain about who we are, now that one of the cornerstones of our realities has crumbled beneath us. We ask ourselves overwhelming questions:

- How can we start over?

- Should we move?

- How can we construct a new social life when we can hardly imagine being with someone new?

We may find ourselves repeating, "If only I had children nearby," reinvoking the mother-hub model of the past; or, "If only I could find a lover," a replay of early romances. It seems sometimes that by magic a chance encounter or sudden event could achieve for us a return to familiar, safe, and orderly lives. Yet the world is neither a particularly generous nor actively hostile place; rather, it is an indifferent one. Only by storing these hopes in the attic of the mind are we free to get on with the building and developing of our lives as they really are.

The first step is to accept the fact that he is really out of your life.

Even going out to get a cup of coffee alone can be a giant symbolic step. Take the case of Phyllis, for example. When her divorce was final, she walked out of her house, which was still full of packing boxes, and went to a nearby diner. As a married family woman, it had never occurred to her to go there. She slid into the booth and ordered, in what she hoped was a casual voice. This act of sitting alone and paying for herself was the first step into a solitary, self-propelled future. That moment of clarity became a reference point as she began the long struggle to form her own life.

If, after a divorce, you wish to change your name, this can also be a powerful symbol of putting away your old identity. It is a great deal of trouble, but the process itself allows some women to think deeply about a fresh start. It means not only making simple changes on stationery, but also making legal applications to change the titles of your Social Security, insurances, credit cards, and passport. The act of changing your name is a way of announcing to your community that you are to be considered anew. It is like a baptism, freeing you to pursue new relationships and recast old friendships that were part of the previous coupling.

Admitting to yourself that you are now alone is a process that will take time. There will be false starts and setbacks. Treat yourself gently during this difficult time, allowing yourself to grieve. Soon you will be ready to move on.

The second step is to build relationships with new people. As we begin to be accustomed to living alone, we face the question of whether to find a sexual partner. At forty or sixty we are looking for something quite different in a partner from what we wanted at twenty. In early adulthood we searched for someone to spend a lifetime with. We considered sexual attractiveness and social appropriateness. We also considered, perhaps unconsciously, whether the man would make a good father. Now, some of these considerations may be irrelevant, as other issues take priority.

Donald and Ruth, for example, found that the crux of their decision to live together had little to do with traditional expectations of sexual satisfaction. Donald's wife, Anna, died after ten years of lingering with Alzheimer's. Twenty years before, Donald and Anna and Ruth and her husband had shared similar academic careers and raised children at the same time. Long divorced, Ruth came to Donald's house during the last five years of the illness to help while Anna's lucidity was failing. Their relationship shifted from that of colleagues and friends to that of co-nurses. Then, as the illness became desperate, they found themselves clinging together for comfort in the face of the horror of watching the death of a person's mind without the death of her body.

When Anna finally had to be institutionalized, Donald and Ruth simply continued to live in the same house, filling each other's lives and finally sharing a bed. They found that they received great pleasure in tender sensuality, in the comfort of hearing each other breathing nearby. Ruth's qualities of earthy practicality balanced Donald's somewhat vague innocence. There seemed to be no reason to marry.

We, too, may discover that we have unusual or unorthodox reasons for choosing a mate. We may choose someone who meets needs very different from those our earlier choices met. If we are especially insecure financially, we may value a solid income; if we are very active physically, we may look for a comparably vital playmate; if we lack intellectual stimulation, we may look for someone with whom to share books, concerts, and conversations. But no matter what we value, if we are done with child rearing, we are free to choose more widely now than we once were. We may wish, then, to redefine ourselves with regard to the range of companions we will allow to become close to us. We may perhaps derive great joy from the company of someone we might once have considered inappropriate, someone perhaps with a very different cultural or ethnic background who can teach us about our own backgrounds by contrast.

If we find ourselves enjoying someone's company, but for some reason assume that "it wouldn't work out," we can stop and examine this. The important question is whether we enjoy being together. In any case, it may be neither possible nor desirable to form as complete an interdependency as we might have when we were younger; we may not wish to marry, for example, or to speak of lifetime commitments.

Consider now, depending on how old you are, what qualities you looked for in a mate when you were

- Twenty?

- Thirty-five?

- Fifty?

- Sixty-five?

What are the major points of difference? Of similarity?

Sometimes the world seems to conspire in wanting us married or remarried. Our well-meaning friends set us up with eligible opposite numbers at dinner parties. No one seems to ask, except those who have arrived at the same threshold, if we would perhaps rather be single, or have a series of lovers with no commitment, or perhaps choose close women friends with whom to share our lives. Our solitary state seems to make some married folks uneasy, especially if their own marriages have become pasteboards of compromise.

Mary, who was just divorced, went to visit a friend living on the Pacific coast of Oregon. The friend was five years into a second marriage that had been made, Mary thought, partially out of her friend's fear of being alone and her desire to avoid the problem of what to do with her life. Mary was experiencing that fine euphoria that sometimes follows divorce: entanglements had been shed, resentments released, golden privacy was deeply enjoyed. During the visit, Mary became aware that being played out in this idyllic setting were the same issues of control that had doomed her own marriage—there were arguments over who handled the money and who drove the car.

One day the husband, in a burst of sympathetic, pitying misunderstanding and arrogance, jokingly suggested to Mary that if she went to a certain beach at a certain time of day, luck might be with her and she might find a husband. In fact, having watched him carp at her friend for a few days, Mary felt she never wanted to marry again. When she tactfully told him this, he was astonished and even hurt, unable to imagine that any woman would prefer a single life.

Suppose now that someone does come into your life. Your longing for touch, sex, companionship, security, and the presence of another person in your house can overwhelm you. In the throes of love, your hard-won independence and clarity about shaping your own destiny may be temporarily swept away. Here are some important questions that may help to evaluate the prospects for long-term success:

- Do you share interests and life-styles?

- How do your energy levels mesh?

- What are your relative financial positions?

- What about the health of each of you?

- If your partner has few or no housekeeping skills, how do you feel about that?

- Do you have fun together?

- What about the eventual responsibility for each of your sets of parents?

- What about the situation of the children, if there are any?

Discouraging answers do not necessarily mean that the relationship is not worth pursuing; rather, they point toward the areas that may be special challenges ahead.

If we are beyond a certain age, the fantasy that a grown-up Prince Charming will sweep us into a passionate romance is, as we all know, highly unlikely statistically. There is a pattern of men choosing younger women, and there are fewer older men than older women because we outlive men by many years. The task here is to become clear about such a fantasy, if it is a powerful one for you. The endless searching and disappointment can sap vitality from the relationships that are available, such as deeper friendships with unavailable men and with other women, and it can close you off to the special stimulation and growth that your solitary status makes available. Furthermore, you may be blaming yourself for your inability to find a partner—but it is not your fault that he is not out there for you. Be honest that you deeply miss having a loving, touching, and caring person in your life. But then let go of that disappointment and move beyond it. Sometimes, when you are focusing elsewhere, romance appears.

At eighty-eight Veronica's mother, Alice, had been widowed for six years. She lived in a "level four" retirement house, for people who can function well but need to be in a semi-protected situation because of physical or mental frailty. Veronica visited her regularly. Alice used a walker and was on a salt-free diet but was sprightly, fully alert, funny, and charming. In the house she made it her business to help other residents, and she was very popular with the staff.

Then Carl, eighty-five, recently widowed and unwilling to cook and shop for himself, arrived as a new resident. He and Alice became friends. They were together every day and soon asked for a change of rooms so they could be next door to each other. The retirement house had no explicit policies about sexual intimacy between residents, but some staff members were clearly uneasy about this "inappropriate" affair. As time went on the couple became more open about their romance,

touching each other affectionately in public. They requested a
larger room so that they could live together.

The director, troubled and anxious to do the right thing,
telephoned Veronica. Her reaction was mixed. She could see
that Alice seemed radiantly content, but she was disturbed at
the image of her ancient mother becoming sexually active.
Distressed, she confronted her mother, asking her to "act her
age."

In the face of this furor, Carl and Alice simply decided to
move to another home, leaving residents, staff, and daughter
to their scruples. They still live happily together, with no
desire to marry. The new home accepts them, perhaps because
they arrived together and the staff and residents were not asked
to deal with a change.

Carl and Alice found love in an unorthodox place at an
unorthodox time, because both were open to it. Their expectations of each other were certainly not those of young lovers,
and they had to defy social and family pressures in order to be
together. So, too, we may remind ourselves that we alone are
the ultimate arbiters of our choices. If our hearts tell us to, we
may move bravely forward, for only we and our partners know
the true texture of what lies between us.

FRIENDSHIPS

Whether we are in a partnership or alone, our friends provide an essential network, giving us affection, stimulation,
learning, and dependable comfort. These relationships can be
enhanced, deepened, and honored. Most of us haven't had
much practice at this. As girls we competed for boyfriends;
then, in the long years of nest building, we focused on family
while friends got whatever time and commitment was left
over. Fortunately, for most of us that archaic pattern of breaking an appointment with a girlfriend to become available for a
date is long past. Think now about your own pattern of friendship.

- Do you have one main friend?

- Or do you stay in touch with several people?

- Do you prefer to have many friends, some closer than others?

- Are most of your friends old ones, kept and cultivated for many years?'

- Do friends and lovers conflict for you in terms of time and energy?

- Or do you feel you maintain a harmonious balance?

We know that our sister-friendships need careful tending. Our friends are our partners in our steps of change. They are the allies who are always there for us, competently and compassionately, when we are in a crisis. Time, thoughtfulness, support, attention, and practical help all cement our commitments and bring reliable and loving others into our lives.

We may, however, have patterns of dealing with friends of which we are not always proud. Perhaps we tend toward great enthusiasm about a new friend, holding out the promise of long intimacy, then our interest fades quickly. Perhaps we spill our troubles to our friends and forget to listen with the same care to them. We may still shortchange them in favor of men or find our conversations or activities together centered around men. Consider now your two closest girlfriends.

- What do you most enjoy doing together?

- How much do you each share about your inner lives and feelings?

- Which one would you call in an emotional crisis?

- Which one would you call for practical help?

- Would this be reciprocal?

- What do you usually talk about?

If close scrutiny of your pattern of making and keeping friends finds you repeating a self-sabotaging behavior or investing less energy in friendships than they need to survive, then the first step is, once again, to become severely and honestly self-critical. Consciously resolve now to make small, manageable changes in your behavior. If you tend toward neglecting your friends, make a point of calling one or two of them this week to find out how *they* are. On the other hand, you may feel that you tend to overwhelm your friends with problems and worries so that the pleasure has gone out of the relationships; you may then want to plan and execute a dinner party, trip to the theater, or hike in the woods with them, just for fun.

Making new friendships may be more difficult for us as adults than it was when we were younger. We are clearer now about our identities, habits, likes, and dislikes and less flexible about accommodating those whom we immediately sense are not for us. Furthermore, we must compensate for the fact that we are probably no longer in school, where we simply found friends because we were together with so many people our own age. We can make a conscious effort to try harder to listen and share, however casually, with someone outside our usual circle. By dismissing people quickly, we are perhaps denying ourselves new knowledge, experience, and companionship.

Sometimes opportunities to meet new people quite literally knock if we can respond to approaches rather than reject them. Betty, for example, a teacher of singing for actors, grew incapacitated by allergies as a young adult and moved to a mountain condominium in Colorado. Although she found part-time work immediately, she felt very cautious socially and couldn't bring herself to approach her new neighbors. She hadn't been there a week before four women came to her door with a welcome wagon, a gift of fruit, bread, and wine. They also brought information about activities within the condominium and the nearby town and the names and telephone numbers of her neighbors. The women were warm and gracious. Betty was particularly drawn to one, who was involved with the theater, like herself. The next day they talked shop over tea, and a third woman came who had once been a costume designer. They found themselves giving birth to a play-reading group. With the help of the welcome wagon, and her own willingness to reach out, Betty had found her way into a new community quite painlessly.

Just as we cannot ask lovers to meet all of our needs and expectations, so we cannot expect one friend to be all things to us. She cannot be the second pair of hands on a wallpapering project as well as the one we call to vent our frustration and grief as well as the ideal concert companion. From a spouse we may, erroneously, expect too many interests and rhythms to mesh with our own; we may more easily appreciate our friends for whatever quality each shares with us. Angela, for example, goes to the theater with Lucy, cooks and eats gourmet meals with Amy, goes shopping with Meg, and travels with Doris. She knows that each friend brings out one aspect of her whole self, some with greater intimacy than others. Yet without any one of them, Lucy, Amy, Meg, or Doris, Angela would be missing a great deal of richness and variety.

Friends with very different life-styles can still enrich each other. Peggy is a productive writer, living alone. She works every day on her personal computer and supports herself. She is soured on marriage and men and is supremely self-reliant. Margaret, on the other hand, has been married for thirty-five years and has never worked outside her home. She is committed to her aging, frail, and forgetful husband. Peggy and Margaret share an enthusiasm for physical projects, a need to save money by doing things themselves, and, since in practice both are without help, a need to tackle difficult household jobs together. Almost every week they do something in each other's houses: they paint, repair and caulk bathroom tiles, refinish furniture, and clean the basements. This becomes a stimulus to work and laughter, as they give each other focus, energy, and the will to finish difficult jobs.

Many of us now alone have been accustomed to body warmth and sexual attention. The absence of touching and being touched is a deep deprivation when we lose our partners. Although there is no replacement for a loving sexual partnership, we still need the touching and holding almost as much now as we did when we were babies.

Many of us probably have some shyness about nonsexual touching. The touch of massage, facials, manicures, and pedicures by professionals may give us this pleasure, but it is a luxury and, after all, the result of a professional relationship. Perhaps there is a friend who might want to exchange massages, shampoos, or foot rubs with you. Aside from saving money and soothing sore muscles, such grooming can meet deeper needs. You may feel embarrassed at first, but that soon fades, and you will improve with practice.

Customs have changed greatly in the way warmth can be-expressed between women. We can now hug each other, cry together, and undress without embarrassment. In some communities it is even perfectly acceptable for women to dance together. The mores have changed, even in brief decades; it is now accepted to honor and cherish our friendships with women.

In adulthood, redefining old relationships and forming new ones require a special openness and willingness to take risks. Our approach is different from that of our early youth. We now know more exactly what we need from a lover or friend. The intensity may be different; our judgment is clearer. Exterior social obligations may seem less imperative, as the quest for a solid, coupled life unfolds with less urgency. Now, as we shift into roles of our own choosing, our question is who *we* are becoming.

□

MINITASKS

We've saved some of the most challenging tasks for last! Do pick and choose among these minitasks, making sure not to try and do too many of these exercises at once.

1 ▪ As a way of reflecting on your partnership, write down three qualities that your partner contributes to your life. For example: humor, sexuality, financial security, intellectual stimulation, companionship, help with projects.

Then write down three important qualities that you think you contribute to your partner's life.

2 ▪ Write down three of your needs that your partner does not meet. For example: company on outings, child-rearing help, help with housework or cooking, intellectual stimulation, exercising companionship.

3 ▪ Identify the need on which you and your partner together could most easily work toward change, and adopt one of the following strategies:

    a. Does your partner know how much this matters to you? If not, find ways of telling him.

    b. Find a balancing area where you may not be meeting your partner's needs, and offer to try to meet them in exchange.

4 ▪ Identify the need that your partner could least easily meet, and adopt these strategies:

    a. Talk to a friend or counselor to get perspective.

b. Take action to find the situation or people outside the partnership who can meet your need, without necessarily seeing this as a threat to the partnership.

5 ▪ Write down three areas in which you believe you do not meet your partner's needs. Choose the one that you feel you could most easily change in yourself, and consciously focus on doing better with this for one week.

6 ▪ If your unmet needs vastly overbalance the needs met in the relationship:

a. Share thoughts and fears about breaking up with a friend or counselor.

b. Read up on any legal aspects to the separation.

c. Tell your partner what you are struggling with, and go together for counseling or mediation if you can.

7 ▪ Who are your two most important friends? Is either one also your lover? How do you distinguish, in your own mind, the qualities of friends and lovers? Write this down in a sentence or two.

8 ▪ Name one valuable friend who lives close by whom you have not been in touch with recently.
Call her this week.
Then name one friend who is far away with whom you have been out of touch for a long time.
Write or call her this week.

9 ▪ Do you know your closest friends' birthdays?
If not, find out and write them in your appointment book for the coming year. Make it a point to do something to mark each.

10 ▪ Have a party for your best women friends.

11 · If you are newly single and living in a new situation, find an excuse to get acquainted with a neighbor (borrow sugar, lose a cat, offer a ride).

12 · If you feel you are alone because of shyness or social awkwardness, join something, anything relatively impersonal, in the next two weeks—the library, volunteering at the hospital, visiting invalids—any activity that connects you gently, if formally, with a new set of faces. If you are healing, then wait. Time is your friend and will let you know when to move outward.

10 · Thresholds

That time counted by anxious worried women
Lying awake, calculating the future,
Trying to unweave, unwind, unravel

And piece together the past and the future,
Between midnight and dawn, when the past is all
    deception,
The future futureless, before the morning watch
When time stops and time is never ending.

T. S. ELIOT

AT EACH OF OUR THRESHOLDS OF CHANGE, WE MADE THE CHOICE
of one path, leaving others unexplored. Each path forked again
and again, and the cumulative effect of these choices is our
life. In these pages we have invited you to reverse this branch-
ing to rediscover paths you might have taken. You may already
have walked new paths as a result of the rethinking you have
done here.

We come full cycle. We integrate the visions of our adolescence into more sophisticated versions of similar dreams.
We begin to make peace with who we have become and to
forgive our shortcomings. We become receptive and alert to
both the outer world and our inner selves, making sense out of
seeming chaos.

As we pass over our life's series of thresholds, time itself
changes shape and meaning. When we were ten the past was

a flickering, brief set of vignettes, with a vast range of choices and rich vistas ahead. At forty we stand evenly between a long past, which we have integrated into patterns and our sense of who we are, and a future replete with options and possible challenges. At seventy the past reaches backward, a rich tapestry of experience and relationships; the future, a time for reflection. Our task, then, is to synthesize all that has gone before, giving ourselves permission to be who we have become, with vigor, laughter, and, for some of us, a joyous disregard for what others think.

Our theme in these pages has been consistent: together we have tried to build a gradual increase in our sense of responsibility for our own choices. We are becoming, in the areas we choose and where life permits, active rather than passive, informed rather than ignorant, sharply aware of our true feelings rather than allowing them to be blurred by obsolete self-descriptions. We approach our futures with renewed attention to our responsibilities to ourselves and others. In the web of the people with whom we live, we are caring and responsive; we compromise as we consciously weigh the issue of freedom versus security.

Visualize now your ideal self as you will be in ten years.

- Where would you be living?

- With whom would you be living, if with anyone?

- Would you have a different profession?

- Would you have learned new things?

- Would your life roles be different?

- In what ways would you have changed?

- What can you begin to change now, inside yourself and in your world, to make such a vision possible?

Imagine yourself once again standing at your current threshold, surveying the paths as they fan out before you. At any point in your life, the new threshold and the many paths will always be there, waiting to be explored. There will always be new quests and challenges, new boundaries to be stretched or reined in. No matter what minitasks you chose for yourself this time, you will choose quite different ones a decade from now.

Certain principles will stay with you:

1.   Choose the path or challenge that is possible and name it clearly.

2.   Start small, and make a firm short-term commitment to the task.

3.   Involve the people important to you in what you are doing.

4.   Replace the "should"s and "ought"s , and find the positive "want to"s in yourself.

5.   Establish a firm knowledge base by reading and asking; become informed.

We end as we began. You have crossed your thresholds, choosing some paths and rejecting others, retreating from some to wait for a better time. You are evolving, not into a different person, but into one whose boundaries have shifted and whose choices have expanded. You stand now upon a different threshold, with new paths beckoning ahead.

Readings

THE FOLLOWING GROUP OF BOOKS LISTED BY CHAPTER INCLUDE titles we think might interest you. Some of the books will help you to delve more thoroughly into a subject, some are wonderful books for you to enjoy, others may give you added information or expertise about a particular area that we have explored together in a chapter.

1. Getting Started

Bernard, Jessie. *Women, Wives and Mothers, Values and Options*. Aldine, 1978.

Brownmiller, Susan. *Femininity*. Fawcett, 1984.

Chernin, Eve. *Remembering Eve: Modern Woman in Search of Herself*. Harper & Row, 1987.

Conway, Jill. *Road from Coorain*. Knopf, 1989.

Readings

Doress, Paula B., and Diana L. Siegal. *Ourselves, Growing Older.* Simon & Schuster, 1987.

Ehrenreich, Barbara, and O. English. *For Her Own Good: 150 Years of the Experts' Advice to Women.* Doubleday, 1979.

Goodman, Ellen. *Turning Points: How People Change Through Crisis and Commitment.* Doubleday, 1979.

Pellegrino, Victoria. *The Other Side of 30: The Breakthrough Decade in a Woman's Life.* Rawson Wade, 1981.

Viorst, Judith. *When Did I Stop Being 20 and Other Injustices.* Simon & Schuster, 1987.

2. Nests and Boundaries

Laver, James. *Costume and Fashion: A Concise History.* Thames & Hudson, 1982.

Lessing, Doris. *The Summer Before the Dark.* Knopf, 1973.

Mannix. *Woman and the Man-made Environment.* Pluto, 1984.

Rubin, Lillian. *Women of a Certain Age: The Midlife Search for Self.* Harper & Row, 1979.

Viorst, Judith. *Necessary Losses.* Fawcett, 1987.

Woolf, Virginia. *A Room of One's Own.* Harcourt, Brace & Jovanovich, 1963.

3. Body Care

Berysenko, Joan. *Minding the Body, Mending the Mind.* Addison-Wesley, 1984.

Boston Women's Health Collective. *The New Our Bodies Ourselves.* Simon & Schuster, 1984.

Brody, Jane. *Jane Brody's Nutrition Book: A Lifetime Guide to Good Eating for Better Health and Weight Control.* Norton, 1981.

Readings

Chernin, Kim. *The Hungry Self: Women, Eating and Identity*. Harper & Row, 1985.

Complete Manual of Fitness and Well-Being: A Lifetime Guide to Self-Improvement. Reader's Digest, 1984.

Freedman, Rita. *Bodylove: Learning to Like our Looks . . . and Ourselves*. Harper & Row, 1989.

Gallop, Jane. *Thinking Through the Body*. Columbia University Press, 1988.

Hasselbring, B., S. Greenwood, and M. Castleman. *The Medical Self-Care Book of Women's Health*. Doubleday, 1987.

Hillman, Howard. *Kitchen Science*. Consumer Reports Books, 1981.

Kano, Susan. *Making Peace with Food: Freeing Yourself from the Diet/Weight Obsession*. Harper & Row, 1985.

McGee, Harold. *On Food and Cooking*. Macmillan, 1984.

Suleiman, Susan. *The Female Body in Western Culture*. Harvard University Press, 1985.

Tannehill, Reah. *History of Food*. Crown, 1989.

Visser, Margaret. *Much Depends on Dinner*. McClelland & Stewart, Toronto, 1987.

Westcott, P., and L. Black. *Alternate Health Care for Women*. Thorsons Public Group, Rochester, Vt., 1987.

4. Money

Chesler, Phyllis, with Jane Goodman. *Women, Money and Power*. William Morrow, 1976.

Klott, Gary. *A Complete Guide to Personal Investing*. New York Times Books, 1987.

Phillips, Michael. *The Seven Laws of Money*. Random House, 1974.

Porter, Sylvia. *Your Financial Security: Effective Strategies for Every Stage of Life.* William Morrow, 1988.

Warschaw, Tessa A. *Rich Is Better.* Doubleday, 1985.

5. Hands, Minds, and Senses

Belenk, Mary F., Blyth M. Clinchy, et. al. *Women's Ways of Knowing: The Development of the Self, Voice and Mind.* Basic Books, 1986.

The Complete Fix-it Manual. Time-Life Books, 1989.

Sandord, Linda, and Mary Donovan. *Women and Self-Esteem: Understanding and Improving the Way We Think and Feel About Ourselves.* Penguin, 1985.

Tetrault, Jeanne, ed. *Women's Carpentry Book.* Anchor, 1980.

Vare, E. A., and G. Ptacek. *Mothers of Invention: From the Bra to the Bomb, Forgotten Women and their Unforgettable Ideals.* William Morrow, 1988.

6. Travel

Davidson, Robin. *Tracks.* Pantheon, 1983.

Fussel, Paul. *The Norton Book of Travel.* Norton, 1987.

Kaye, Dena. *Traveling Woman.* Bantam, 1981.

Newby, Eric, ed. *The Book of Travelers' Tales.* Penguin, 1987.

Morris, Mary. *Nothing to Declare: Memoirs of a Woman Traveling Alone.* Houghton Mifflin, 1988.

7. Loneliness and Solitude

Buber, Martin. *I and Thou.* Scribner's, 1936.

Heilbrun, Carolyn. *Writing a Woman's Life.* Ballantine, 1989.

Sarton, May. *Journal of a Solitude.* Norton, 1973.

Storr, Anthony. *Solitude: A Return to the Self.* Macmillan, Free Press, 1988.

Tillich, Paul. *The Courage to Be.* Yale University Press, 1977.

8. Renewing the Past: Relationships with Parents

Fox, Nancy. *You, Your Parent and the Nursing Home: The Family Guide to Long-Term Care.* Geriatric Press, Bend, Ore., 1986.

Friday, Nancy. *My Mother, My Self.* Delacorte Press, 1977.

Jarvik, Lissy, and Gary Small. *Parentcare: A Commonsense Guide for Adult Children.* Crown, 1988.

Nassif, Janet Zhun. *The Home Health Care Solution.* Harper & Row, 1985.

Payne, Karen, ed. *Between Ourselves: Letters Between Mothers and Daughters, 1750–1982.* Houghton Mifflin, 1983.

Sarton, May. *A Reckoning.* Norton, 1978.

9. Relationships: Lovers and Friends

de Beauvoir, Simone. *The Second Sex.* Random House, 1974.

Dinnerstein, D. *The Mermaid and the Minotaur: Sexual Arrangement and Human Malaise.* Harper & Row, 1976.

Eidenbaum, L., and S. Orbach. *Between Women: Love, Envy and Competition in Women Friendships.* Viking, 1987.

Lerner, Harriet G. *The Dance of Anger: A Women's Guide to the Changing Patterns of Intimate Relationships.* Harper & Row, 1989.

Pogrebin, Letty. *Among Friends.* McGraw-Hill, 1987.

Acknowledgments

We gratefully acknowledge the suggestions, support, and contributions of the following people:

Julian Bach, Vicky Bijur, Chris Bohley, Anne Eberle, Adam Garfinkle, Priscilla Grayson, Christine Forsyth, Anne Judson, Liang Heng, Louella Hotsenpillar, Peter Keepnews, Don Korn, Barbara Lawrence, William Lederer, Alan Luxenberg, Adria-ann MacMurray, Kate Mostkoff, Anne Plunkett, Debra Putnam, Ann Rittenberg, Ellen Shapiro, Mark Shapiro, Priscilla Skerry, Lynne Smith, Susanne Weiss, Ann White, and especially Jane von Mehren, our patient editor.